# CHANGING WAYS

A Practical Tool for Implementing
Change Within Organizations

Murray M. Dalziel
Stephen C. Schoonover

American Management Association

*This book is available at a special
discount when ordered in bulk quantities.
For information, contact Special Sales Department,
AMACOM, a division of American Management Association,
135 West 50th Street, New York, NY 10020.*

**Library of Congress Cataloging-in-Publication Data**

Dalziel, Murray.
  Changing ways.

    Includes index.
    1. Organizational change.  2. Leadership.
I. Schoonover, Stephen C., 1947-      .
II. Title.
HD58.8.D34  1988        658.4'063        87-40501
ISBN 0-8144-5924-2

*Printing number*

*10 9 8 7 6 5 4 3 2*

# Preface

*Changing Ways* is for all of us who live every day with the promises that change can bring. For some people, change is stimulating, a real adventure. For others, it is painful and anxiety-provoking. Yet the stark reality of today's business world is that no one can avoid change. This book is designed to help you make change efforts productive, even exciting, for yourself, colleagues, clients, and coworkers.

The ideas in this book began to take shape about ten years ago when a major industrial corporation approached McBer and Company with a problem. The leaders in the corporation were dissatisfied with the rate at which automation was being introduced in their plants. Despite their leadership in several aspects of factory automation, the company experienced as many failures as successes. There was obviously more to success than technological leadership. This led one of the authors to study the reasons why some change implementations work well and others don't. The study revealed significant differences between the ways successful and less successful organizations dealt with the human and organizational aspects of change.

The results of the factory automation study intrigued us. One of us has spent the last 12 years in various projects helping large organizations change. The other has combined a clinical practice helping individuals change their lives with an interest in how organizations change. Our combined interests and the initial findings about a factory automation change project led us to investigate the factors that determine success in other types of change, such as new quality programs, organizational redesigns, introducing MIS systems, office automation, or new personnel systems. *Changing Ways* crystallizes the findings of these studies, focusing on the vital processes that effective leaders of change use to overcome the inevitable resistance that accompanies their efforts.

## WHO SHOULD READ *CHANGING WAYS*?

This book is for *Change leaders*. Unfortunately, "change leader" is not part of any job description. So, how do you know if you are a change leader or should be one? We have found that change leaders have one thing in common—they are concerned about the details of the change *process*. They recognize that change from inception through its implementation has consequences beyond the initial objectives. For example, the introduction of personal work stations often makes an organization reevaluate the role of an administrative assistant. In manufacturing, implementing Material Requirement Planning Systems causes organizations to reexamine how engineering and production should be coordinated. New incentive systems often generate new concerns about the outcomes management expect from people.

These types of consequences have ramifications for all levels of an organization. If you are a senior executive, you know that your role is most often *sponsorship* of change so that your organization can continue to compete in the modern world. However, like many senior executives, you may be frustrated by how difficult it is to get people to buy into change efforts. For you, *Changing Ways* offers a set of standards to speed up implementation by ensuring that common human and organizational barriers do not obstruct change efforts.

If you are a middle-level manager, you must live through and with the day-to-day consequences of any change. Yet at your level, in today's business climate, the ability to implement change effectively is often the difference between overall success and failure. For you, *Changing Ways* provides a personal road map to increase your skills at planning, managing, and implementing change.

If you are a technical specialist or an individual contributor, you are at the heart of most change efforts. Although there is a tendency in management literature to equate leadership with management roles, in most change efforts this is far from true. We have observed many change leaders who are individual contributors, including systems analysts, manufacturing engineers, and personnel specialists. They carry out the technical details of a project; they tailor them to the needs of the people who have to live with the change—the "end users." The very best technical specialists make change a success by attending to the human and organizational aspects of the change process. If you are a technical specialist, *Changing Ways* will complement your technical skills and offer you ways to become more personally effective in your vital role.

## HOW *CHANGING WAYS* IS ORGANIZED

*Changing Ways* is organized in three parts:

*Part I* (Chapters 1-3) discusses the change process in general and how you can begin to develop a leadership approach that will maximize your impact on the organization.

*Part II* (Chapters 4-6) is the core of the book, describing the major factors that produce successful change efforts. In this section you will learn practical steps to:

- Ensure that your organization is prepared for specific change efforts,
- Obtain the right mix of skills on projects, and
- Avoid the common pitfalls during implementation.

*Part III* (Chapters 7-8) provides guidelines for integrating strategies for change and suggests ways you can use our findings to transform both organizations and individuals.

Since people learn in different ways, we have designed the book to accommodate a variety of learning styles. Each chapter offers case examples, narrative descriptions of skills, summary sections, and an exercise you can use to sharpen your use of our suggestions. We have intentionally provided materials to benefit both cover-to-cover readers and skimmers.

We use a variety of examples and cases from our consulting experience, while being careful to protect the anonymity of clients. Any reference to a company name was obtained from generally available information.

Regardless of how you use *Changing Ways*, it should serve as a practical tool for implementing change. Because of the rapid political, economic, social, and technological changes that are occurring in the world around us, planning and implementing innovations is not only a topic of great interest but also a necessity for business and personal career survival. Change also provides great opportunities. We hope that *Changing Ways* will help you realize these possibilities.

## ACKNOWLEDGEMENTS

*Changing Ways* was developed by the efforts of many individuals. Nicholas Weiler stimulated our initial interest in the topic and over the years his insight into what really works in organizations has been very helpful. William Kraus was a valuable colleague in applying the findings in their early stages.

Our colleagues at McBer and Company have challenged and refined our thinking. In particular, our discussions with Richard Boyatzis, James Burruss, Mary Esteves, Don Payne, Robert Ryan, Lyle Spencer, and Helen Vandkjaer stimulated and clarified many of the ideas presented in the book.

Tom Burke and Richard Morse read early drafts and provided us with direction about the needs of those who have to manage change in business settings.

Our spouses, Elizabeth Rogers and Ellen Bassuk, have been patient, and tolerant, of our schedules. We also have benefited greatly from their professional help. In addition, Mary Nell Schoonover significantly rewrote and edited major sections. Not many authors are fortunate enough to have an editor who has also been a successful senior executive. Without her help, we would not have been able to translate research findings into a practical perspective.

Finally, we owe a debt to our clients. One of the things that continues to stimulate us as consultants is our interactions with you. We hope that we have captured the essence of what you have shared with us about your everyday experiences in the changing business world.

Murray M. Dalziel

September 1987

Stephen C. Schoonover

# CONTENTS

# PART I

## CHANGE LEADERSHIP

# CHAPTER 1

# Making Change Happen—
# An Introduction

Change is a pervasive aspect of our lives and almost a necessity for economic survival. In the present business environment there are people to whom change happens and people who like to make it happen. Referred to as *change leaders*, these are the individuals who are responsible for the *process* of change. If you are in this category, this book is for you.

You may be responsible for various types of change—all organizations have people who sponsor, manage, or implement change. However, "leader" is an appropriate title for all individuals who ensure that the change brings maximum benefit to their organizations. By following the practices in this book, you can improve your own change leadership and guide your organization to introduce change more effectively.

Organizational changes can take many forms. They may encompass *hard* systems, such as factory automation or a new computer system; or a *soft* area, such as personnel or quality systems. In addition, some changes are on a large scale, such as organizational structuring; some are small in scale, such as the introduction of personal work stations in a department. These changes all have one thing in common: they can be planned.

3

If you are one of today's leaders, you have already experienced the rapid change in modern business. For instance, in the U.S. automobile industry, 35 percent of the market has been lost to foreign competition in the last ten years. Manufacturing businesses have seen a similar 25 percent loss. Fast-paced industries such as telecommunications or information processing are being transformed by the introduction of lasers and fiber optics. Biotechnology promises to do the same for very stable commodity industries, such as plastics or fertilizers, over the next decade. In the United States service sector jobs have increased almost three times faster than in the manufacturing sector. In the business office of six years ago, there were few multipurpose work stations; now there are over ten million personal computers in American offices. An increase by over 150 percent is expected during the next four years.

But, as a change leader, you also know another side to this fast-changing environment—uncertainty. For instance, factory automation, robotics, and flexible manufacturing all hold great promise. Nevertheless, although there have been a great many technological advances in these areas in the last five years, the rate of expansion has been less than the promises of the 1970s. As a manager in one of the leading automobile manufacturers remarked, "There are fewer advanced manufacturing facilities today than we expected in the seventies, because we have not learned how to overcome people's resistance to these changes."

The fast pace of change is disturbing to many people. Although there are a number of reasons for their distress, technology lovers frequently blame psychological or emotional factors. In contrast, as a more honest manager of a high-tech firm reported, "The disruptions that change brings are overemphasized. More often technological change is painful because those driving the change are design engineers who design for the people they know best—that's right, design engineers." These are harsh words from a fellow design engineer. However, many wise implementors of organizational change echo a similar concern—that changes suit the change makers, not necessarily the people who have to live with them.

If change is both a necessity for survival and a potentially painful experience, how can you as the change leader develop the most appropriate focus or approach? Too often consultants and theorists latch onto the latest hot topic or fad and suggest global strategies or quick fixes for organizational maladies. Even worse, "popularizers" repackage simple truths into new commandments for sure success or take the latest success story—a chicken mogul, pizza king, or computer whiz—and make sweeping generalizations about how to leverage yourself and your business into the top echelon of the Fortune 500. It is human nature to want heroes and simple paths to follow.

The unique stories that chronicle how individuals succeed in changing their organizations do touch on the faith and initiative required for conceiving and implementing innovations. Unfortunately, they do not clarify *the best practices* for achieving success. In fact today's victories can become tomorrow's defeats when individuals in organizations copy the successes of one-time interventions.

The basic problem with most recent studies of "excellence" or "innovation" is that they focus only on the factors that led their successful companies to that point. How do the authors of these studies know that these factors are the cause of success? Unless you also study average companies you cannot really discover the features that *distinguish* successful from less successful organizations. The characteristics that you may find in common between average organizations and successful companies are minimum requirements for survival. Only the factors that distinguish successful from less successful organizations give a strategic advantage to those who adopt them.

To be successful in today's environment you should not base strategy either on a one-time success or on practices employed by both outstanding and average companies. You must be distinctive. The studies that led to the results reported in *Changing Ways* focused on the factors that distinguish successful from less successful change endeavors. We initially concentrated on factory automation, assessing companies (or units of large multinational companies) that more successfully adopted or installed automated machinery than comparable units. Later, when we looked at the introduction of quality programs, we again measured differences in success between similar units. In a variety of additional studies (ranging from new MIS systems to organizational changes), we used similar measures to assess the factors that produce successful planned change.

Our method for generating excellence focused on the best behaviors of the best leaders. In extensive interviews we concentrated not only on what people thought was important but on *what they actually did.* Trained interviewers helped people to "relive" change experiences by reviewing what really happened, who the participants were, how they related to coworkers, and how they perceived the outcomes of a variety of situations in the change process. By taping the interviews and systematically analyzing them with objective criteria, we generated *those factors that produce results* in planned change.

We should be clear about what *Changing Ways* will and will not do. Although planned changed and innovation demand creativity, our intention is not to prescribe directly how to *become creative.* Rather, we focus on *how to harness, express, and apply the creativity* that already exists in an organization.

Also, some experts focus primarily on methods for getting people to *formulate change efforts.* We focus instead on *how* to change—the method to use—rather than *what* to change. Although others highlight what should be changed and what should be preserved in an organization, our approach is oriented toward implementations that test and refine change initiatives and generate new change efforts.

Some books concentrate on a *scope of change,* including the total economic environment and how this should be managed. They frequently offer advice for the future. *Changing Ways* is not filled with predictions for the future, for example, the nature of the next "oil crisis," nor does it advise how to prepare for coming events. Instead, it offers a *method for implementing change,* once you have decided on a course of action. Instead of giving pronouncements about change, we propose ways to ensure that you can smoothly transform any process, procedure, or organizational realignment.

Managing the inevitable stress of change is a prerequisite for organizational growth. Some authorities describe how you can help people *adapt* or respond positively to change. Most of these approaches are loosely defined or impractical, requiring fundamental changes in attitudes or personalities. We use a different approach that is much more practical. By offering straightforward practices and a framework for change, change leaders can provide productive directions for others to follow while calming concerns. By showing exactly how to apply the behaviors of the best performers, *Changing Ways* provides both a road map for analyzing and planning a change process and a change leader's guide to improving personal and organizational effectiveness.

# CHAPTER 2

# A Framework for Change

*Change initiatives can be accomplished by using
a framework for organizational diagnosis,
problem solving, planning, and generating
implementation strategies.*

## WHAT IS CHANGE?

*Change* has become one of the most used and abused buzz words of the 1980s. But what is it and why do it? A 55-year-old worker of a midwestern manufacturing company wrote this response on an attitude survey:

> Every day of my life I see things change. I know I'm changing too. I'm not getting any younger. The people in my neighborhood are changing. A lot of things at work are changing. But I get worried when our new CEO comes to town talking about the need for "dynamic change." They say he's got "vision," but I think our product is stable and solid. It comes from over 20 years of doing the same thing. People appreciate our stability. So why should we change anyway?

We know that successful businesses must provide a stable environment in order to be productive. They also must adapt constantly to new market pressures, changing customers, new information and technologies, and shifting practices and processes inside the organization. But what is the best way to change?

Change can be defined as a planned or unplanned response of an organization to pressures. These can stem from a variety of sources—individuals, teams, coalitions, and interest groups both inside or outside the organization. It may result in or be the result of a new attitude, such as the current focus on quality of work life, or an idea, such as participative management. It may be reflected in new work procedures, policies, processes, or products. It always embodies new functions and relationships among employees. For example, "just-in-time" manufacturing procedures that result in decreased inventories require an increase in work coordination. As a result, more effective teamwork, often launched through new organizational programs such as quality circles, must go hand-in-hand with changes in manufacturing practices.

Change may result from the outside environment in the form of new competition, new social values, or new business practices. In all its forms, change creates opportunities and vulnerabilities. Worldwide financial services have been transformed as a result both of deregulation and information systems offering consumers a whole range of products that would have been inconceivable ten years ago. Although these shifts have offered great potential, the most successful institutions have been able both to see opportunities and implement change. As one marketing manager of a bank told us, "One of the biggest customer service problems leading consumers to switch accounts to competitors is the failure of automatic tellers to function correctly." In practice, those organizations that implemented these systems gained significant market share over those that did not.

Although change is painful for businesses, the result is often a better, more streamlined organization. This has been particularly true in large commodity industries, such as steel or chemicals. As costs rose in some sectors and the supply increased almost as fast, the winners were either able to move into highly profitable, specialized sectors or were able to reduce costs to gain price advantage. Whatever the strategy, it required significant organizational and technological restructuring for successful implementors to win.

Change is an attitude, a state of mind, a stance. But the stance of some leaders can cause unexpected trouble during change efforts. Three specific leadership stances can result in problems—*visionary, technocratic,* and *sympathetic.*

Visionary leaders often view change as a necessary process that emanates from sweeping *cultural* shifts. Proponents of this perspective frequently make global pronouncements that stimulate action before a thorough consideration of eventual consequences. Visions need structure. One CEO lamented that three weeks after he had made a major speech about the orientation of the company, middle managers were asking for clarity about the direction in which the company was going. After further examination we found that the middle managers accepted the vision, but wanted to know what this vision meant to them in their day-to-day jobs.

Technocratic leaders, on the other hand, focus exclusively on outcomes without considering the concerns of employees who must implement and sustain change. They become so seduced by project technicalities that processes and feelings are seen as obstacles. As one manager noted, "People resist anyway. Your only recourse is to push change through aggressively." This perspective frequently results in short-term gains, unforeseen pitfalls, and long-term resentments.

In contrast to technocratic leaders, sympathetic leaders devote too much attention to people and how they feel about change. This style can have the opposite effect from the technocratic style. It freezes momentum. After some time employees beg for leadership and guidance, not sympathy and understanding.

Each of these stances toward change—visionary, technocratic and sympathetic—are presented as extremes. Although these attitudes are often an attempt at coping with the uncertainties that change spawns, each can undermine the vital steps of planning required for the *process of change.*

Because change is a process, events—often unexpected events—unfold over time. In its most raw and destructive form, change is chaos, decay, a loss of control, frequently resulting in more problems than opportunities or advantages. For example, a few years ago, the *New York Times* reported a story about Chinese soldiers billeted on an island in the South China Sea known for its bird fertilizers. While guarding the island, the soldiers brought chickens to provide meat and eggs. On arrival, the chickens literally flew the coop and disappeared. In the process of recapturing the chickens, the soldiers discovered large predatory rats that were eating the chickens and their eggs. They figured they had to take care of the rat problem or they wouldn't have any chickens. So, they ordered a bunch of cats from the mainland and set them loose. Unfortunately, the cats preferred chasing chickens and the birds that produced fertilizer more than the rats. Now the soldiers had a cat problem. So, they ordered dogs from the mainland to control the cats. Unfortunately, the dogs not only couldn't catch the cats, but they also barked constantly and fought with one another. A follow-up article in the *Times* reported that the soldiers still had the rat problem, and the cat problem, and the dog problem, and still no chickens or fresh eggs.

Fortunately, most changes do not have quite the impact of the Chinese government's efforts. There are more commonplace examples. In one company, robots, installed on the assembly line, transformed the manufacturing operation from a standard batch facility to a continuous process operation. However, since the time required for work in that area was always based on piece rates, significant problems resulted until the rate structure for the remaining workers was renegotiated. Another corporation created a career development program for young, fast-track engineers. Everyone thought it was a good idea. But, implementors were shocked by the level of resistance encountered in the field as managers worried about the nonproductive time required to run the program and the prospect of developing and then losing talented employees.

In a very real sense, change often is a prerequisite for organizational survival. One company, building nuclear reactors around the world, realized that in view of public attitudes about nuclear energy, the demand for new reactors would decline rapidly. Therefore, they would have to alter their business strategy radically. After a lot of thought and discussion, they realized that the care and servicing of existing reactors was a business in which they could take a prime position. Consequently, they completely reorganized their direction. This involved substantial changes in the engineering, manufacturing and commercial functions. Moreover, it required a fundamental realignment in the attitude of everyone in the organization to become a provider of services to companies who possessed reactors, rather than a producer of reactors.

## PLANNING FOR CHANGE

One of the primary responsibilities of leadership is to organize activities. This always requires *building blocks* or principles and behaviors that are used to form a coherent set of steps for action. The processes described in this book can be used as a planning tool. They not only can anchor specific change efforts but can ensure that an appropriate level of energy and resources are allocated for using change as a competitive strategy.

The methods we discuss are ideal for initiating *hard* changes, such as robotics or computerizing a warehouse, or new systems, such as a communication network or automated office. However, they are just as necessary and just as effective for implementing *soft* changes, such as new safety practices or a new quality program. Even large-scale organizational changes in the form of mergers, organizational redesigns, restructuring of reporting relationships, or new policies and procedures, need ongoing planning. Although the range and scope of change in today's corporations offer unique opportunities, they also require organization and control by change leaders.

All too often, organizational change is guided by reactive initiatives or wishful visions, rather than planning based on sound principles. For example, a major reprographics company redirected its corporate strategy toward information technology and office automation. They wanted to be the technological leaders in the "office of the future." Therefore, they developed a leading-edge local area network, the best in photocopiers and electronic publishing systems, and a diverse array of superior work stations. However, they put so much emphasis on new, leading-edge technology that they missed the fact that a great deal of the personal work-station market had adopted the IBM-PC as a standard. Their research center is known as one of the leaders in computer science, but the practicality of the IBM-PC world eluded them. They did develop a non-IBM compatible personal computer that was poorly advertised. To date, the result has been a superior vision and excellent product line with no anchor in a PC-driven marketplace. On the other hand, another computer firm built its success and image in carefully planned small steps by taking IBM's success in establishing the standard in office work stations and providing a better IBM compatible computer than IBM.

In today's competitive environment, organizational change is universal, pervasive, necessary. However, the attitudes and practices of individual leaders determine whether or not change is productive or destructive. In our experience with change projects, three basic attitudes about change generally predominate during planned innovations:

- "I'm not sure how to change; besides things are going pretty well—the status quo may be better anyway."
- "Everybody gets frustrated by change; you just have to ignore the frustrations and push ahead or you won't get anything done."
- "You need to change; you have to change; in fact, I'd get bored if we weren't trying out new things."

Even though these outlooks are both inevitable and valid, the most successful change leaders resist the tendency to adopt usual group attitudes. Instead, they assume a fourth stance based on proactive planning. For example, one successful change leader captured the attitude of best performers: "I know we need to change, but I know it's not magic, or inspiration. It's completing many, many, undramatic small steps successfully."

## CONFRONTING VULNERABLE AREAS
## OF THE CHANGE PROCESS

Effective change leaders deal with the tangible and hidden processes of change by answering three key questions about the change effort:

- Have we got our organization *ready* for planned change?
- Do we have *the right mix of skills* on our team to make the change happen?
- Can we ensure that the *implementation process* will be successful?

In Chapters 4-6 we define the behaviors that encompass these three areas—*organizational readiness, change-team roles,* and *the implementation process* and define the attributes that assure successful change efforts. Since our research captures the factors that distinguish the best from average change efforts, you can use our findings as a guide to assess your organization's strengths and vulnerabilities or as a set of strategies for solving problems and confronting weaknesses that interfere with effective change.

The three key questions also encompass *the natural time span required for a change project.* First, change leaders have to prepare their organization for change. Next, they have to ensure that they have the right people working with them. And finally, as they pass from the idea stage, through development, toward implementation, they must follow an action plan that ensures their organization can embrace and absorb the change.

Chapter 4 explores Organizational Readiness. There are five attributes of organizational readiness.

- *History of Change*: The prior experience of the organization in accepting change.
- *Clarity of Expectations*: The degree to which the expected results of change are shared across various levels of the organization.

- *Origin of the Idea or Problem*: The degree to which those most affected by the change initiated the idea or problem the change solves.
- *Support of Top Management*: The degree to which top management sponsors the change.
- *Compatibility with Organizational Goals*: The degree to which the proposed change corresponds to past and present organizational practices and plans.

The first three dimensions—*history of change, clarity of expectations,* and *origin of the request or problem*—focus on how to *motivate* people to embrace change. To stimulate a positive attitude toward change, change leaders let "success breed success", by scaling initial interventions to their organization's past performance. As one change leader aptly stated, "The most important thing is not to fail at the start. You should always ensure an initial success—even if you have to move more slowly or only start a small part of the change." In addition, change leaders share information with those most affected by change to instill consistent expectations about the change and its ramifications throughout the organization. Finally, they make sure that the change is framed to meet key problems of those who will have to live with the change first.

A financial organization, seeking to create a completely new set of procedures to compete for a new line of business, delayed the restructuring, because the targeted division had low morale and a very poor history of change. In fact, its senior management had been fired in previous months. In this context, senior management believed that any proposal to change strategic direction would be met with even more resistance. To cope with the problem, the bank created a special unit within one of the branches to test the new product. Implementors from the special unit reported the results at regular monthly meetings. At the end of one of the meetings, someone excluded from the initial pilot, suggested that "it was stupid not to be doing this across the whole division!" Others in the division concurred. Thereafter, senior management "relented" to their demands by initiating a plan that would bring everyone into the system over time. As one senior manager said afterwards, "It was a pleasant surprise to have changed from being the big, bad people pushing change to taking the role of resisting the change they wanted."

*Support of top management* is critical at the initial stages of planned change and important throughout the process. Upper-level alliances provide tangible support in the form of resources for various phases of the project and intangible support in the form of sponsorship and networking. However, implementors and middle-level managers frequently ignore this crucial step in their desire to push change. In some ways this is quite natural, since it contradicts the action-oriented bias of traditional management. As one middle-level manager put it, "I am told that the only way to succeed is to take initiative, to look as if I'm in control. Yet I need top-level sponsorship to successfully implement my programs." Leaders managing successful endeavors generate upper-level support much more often than those producing less successful results, because they recognize the political realities of organizational life. Independent control is necessary for day-to-day activities. However, when significant resources must be expended, other factions in an organization must be mobilized. That usually requires top-level support.

We also found that the behaviors of top management were a key factor in determining the success of planned innovations. For example, in the most effective change projects, top management actively participated in solving problems throughout the life span of the process. In less successful efforts, they often played a limited role as "providers of capital."

*Compatibility with organizational goals* is an attribute of change initiatives that defines how well change goals correspond with other ongoing processes in the organization, such as values, policies, and business practices. The best change leaders tailor the scope, scale, and type of change to fit existing patterns. This keeps the effort practical. One manager told us, "We kept telling our people how we wanted to achieve quality standards. It was only when we took them with some customers to another division of our company that things changed. Over there, workers showed us exactly how that division produced quality. This demonstration got everyone on board, because they could see how it fit work practices they understood."

*Choosing the right people for the implementation team is another critical aspect of the change process* that we will examine in more detail in Chapter 5. Since a wide range of individual skills are required for the various aspects of change, who should be selected for the team and what function should they perform? The most successful change efforts used an array of team configurations. Some teams worked collaboratively; some had an identified leader; some were formal; some were networks that seldom met together, if ever. Some included many members; some had a few people performing multiple functions. In all cases, however, the teams "covered" the functions of the following six roles:

- *Inventor*: Integrates trends and data into concepts, models, and plans; envisions the "big picture" first; adapts plans.
- *Entrepreneur*: Instinctively focuses on organizational efficiency and effectiveness; identifies critical issues and new possibilities; actively seeks advantages and opportunities.
- *Integrator*: Forges alliances; gains personal acceptance, as well as acceptance of the team and their program; relates practical plans to strategic plans and organizational issues.
- *Expert*: Takes responsibility for the technical knowledge and skills required for the change; uses information skillfully and explains it in a logical way.
- *Manager*: Simplifies, delegates, assigns priorities; develops others; gets the job done at all costs.
- *Sponsor*: Ensures support and resources from the highest levels of the organization; communicates where the change fits in the overall organizational "vision."

In practice, *role coverage* is the factor that ensures success. In other words, a group of individuals must perform the key behaviors or skills of each role. *Who* fills the role is of little importance. For example, people often serve simultaneously as the *inventor* and the *entrepreneur* to provide ideas and energy for getting the whole project going. The inventor's ideas and the entrepreneur's ability to marshal resources for the project are both prerequisite for initiating change. In contrast, change efforts need an *expert* and *manager* to ensure that the project will work at a functional level. The roles of *integrator* and the *sponsor* help to keep implementors focused and motivated. They overcome the inevitable organizational barriers imposed by end users.

Change leaders understand which role or roles they can perform competently and how to select others for the remaining roles. This requires honest self-appraisal, particularly about personal limitations, and the skillful assessment of others. Beyond building a team with the potential to fulfill the six roles, change leaders ensure that the roles *operate* throughout the change process. For example, a very competent young engineer diligently worked to install a robot as part of the company's established automation plan. Because he was so engrossed in the technical details of the project, he didn't inform anyone about exactly what he was doing or when he would be finished. One day he arrived with the robot's company engineer to do the "final installation." The plant manager was enraged; he had just put the critical piece of machinery in the repair shop for maintenance. The shop steward and industrial relations manager were enraged; they had never been consulted about when the installation was to take place, even though notification of an installation date was part of the company's union negotiations, The most senior technical manager on the shop floor was also enraged, because he wanted to know why the young engineer's manager hadn't been in touch. The young engineer had done an excellent job. The robot worked to perfection. The project was completed on time. But everyone was furious.

These kinds of problems, sometimes labeled "poor communications," most often stem from critical role deficits. A sponsor was needed to ensure that adequate resources were available and that problems were prioritized to enable the manager to focus on the right thing at the right time. A manager was needed to generate a clear plan, a schedule, and milestones that the engineer could follow. An integrator was needed to see that all the different factions were informed and that conflicts were surfaced and confronted prior to final installation.

Leaders often overlook the need to prepare their organization for change and to develop effective change-team roles. Most leaders try to make concrete plans. However, they frequently omit vital steps or dimensions required for success.

*The Implementation Stage of planned change ensures that goals are completed.* These are the critical factors, which we will explore further in Chapter 6:

- *Clarifying Plans* is the process in which implementors define, document, and specify the change.
- *Integrating New Practices* is the process in which an organization incorporates change into its operations.
- *Providing Education* includes those programs in which end users learn about and use new processes and procedures.
- *Fostering Ownership* is the process through which end users come to identify new processes and procedures as their own, rather than regarding them as changes imposed upon them.
- *Giving Feedback* is the process in which a detailed objective is monitored and used to judge the effectiveness of the implementation plan.

The first three components—*clarifying plans, integrating new practices,* and *providing education*—are the main vehicles for making the change functional. Effective change leaders specify clear plans that have *moderate risk*—challenging enough to stretch employees and sustain motivation, feasible enough to produce results within a realistic time frame. They also break change into steps that can be understood and performed easily and provide enough educational resources to fulfill the learning needs of end users.

A manager who was responsible for a major quality initiative reported, "We had a large chart up on the office wall specifying what the quality initiative was going to do. There was a map showing which areas of the organization were going to be tackled first. We started with the easiest first—material handling. Of course, first, we put all the senior managers through the quality circles course, so they would know how to embrace the program as we implemented it."

Motivating people to change remains an ongoing challenge throughout the change process. Two key dimensions of implementation, *fostering ownership* and *giving feedback,* are key dimensions for sustaining or rejuvenating motivation and commitment. For example, effective leaders involve others and provide concrete and visible outcomes for people as soon as possible after implementation starts. A CEO of a major international bank reported, "We got the automated tellers up and running in record time. So, I had a celebration to reward the staff. The staff liked it well enough, but what surprised me most was the way my team couldn't wait to come to my weekly reporting meeting on how many people were using the tellers and how they were affecting branch performance." The bank CEO's approach illustrates the difference between a one-time reward and a feedback loop or process that demonstrates how interventions are producing results.

It is important, however, to understand that every successful change has its own unique set of problems, complaints, and resistances. Indeed, encompassing these is a key both to *setting the stage* and *sustaining the momentum* during change efforts. In addition, implementors need to examine the results they wish to achieve before starting the change process. The most common, general expectations are

- The change effort will be generally accepted,
- The program will be implemented close to schedule,
- The cost of the undertaking will be close to budget, and
- Whatever is changed will perform close to what the system implementors initially proposed.

To be successful a change endeavor should resemble the original intentions of its implementors. In some change efforts, however, these intentions drift. An engineering system, for example, was withdrawn after eighteen months of sitting idle in one business of a multinational corporation. In spite of this, it is now being used successfully by another section. The company can claim it has a return on its investment, although not as fast as it predicted. This cannot be called a successful change effort, because the outcome does not resemble what the implementors originally intended.

Change leadership has a built-in structure for guaranteeing that results of the change effort will fulfill original objectives. By using its dimensions as a framework for planning and organizing change, leaders can significantly increase the success of implementation.

## MAKE IT PERSONAL

The best way to understand how to improve a planned change is to apply some of the success factors. Think of a successful planned change in which you have been involved and review the following questions to assess how and why the change effort succeeded.

1.   What were some high points during the change effort?
     What issues around organizational readiness, the change team, or implementation were employed?

2.   What were some low points during the change effort?
     What success factors were missing?
     How could applying them have improved the situation?

3.   Which of the four success criteria did the change meet?

- Was it generally accepted?
- Was it implemented close to schedule?
- Was the cost of the undertaking close to budget?
- Is whatever was changed performing close to what the system implementors claimed at the start?

4. Considering organizational readiness, the change team, and implementation success factors, what would you consider doing differently for future changes?

# CHAPTER 3

# What Change Leaders Do

*Change is an inevitable process, harnessed for competitive advantage, by leaders who master the behaviors of the best change implementors.*

## CHANGE LEADERS ARE DOERS

Change leadership is about harnessing and controlling the potential chaos and distress that comes with change. In the most innovative companies, leaders consistently demonstrate a "take-charge—can-do" attitude. They repeatedly overcome the unexpected difficulties with change. In less successful change efforts, managers often overlook the most obvious and critical barriers. In the excitement of focusing on change goals, they may become blinded to their environment and new problems that arise with each step in the change process.

A change represents the synthesis of goals and strategies for achieving an objective, but it needs a driver—the change leader. Chapter 2 introduced a framework for organizing innovation into a plan. The plan, however, is only a group of *possibilities,* a piece of paper with tentative commitments. *Effective leaders ensure that possibilities become realities.* They track both the stated and unstated requirements of a plan, giving each aspect, formal and informal, vigorous scrutiny. For example, a systems engineer described how he launched a change:

> We included what is called a "live test" as part of our plan. We put a robot out in an area of the shop floor. This allowed people to come and look and touch it. At first, they only asked some questions. For example, they wanted to know why it looked more like an octopus than a person. Within a couple of days, they were giving the robot cigarettes to handle. Their acceptance was more important than the actual system test. They became convinced they could live with a robot that could light cigarettes!

How do the best change leaders cope with the stress and confusion change brings? In some ways, they are the true heroes of today's organizations, since they translate the innovative spirit into useful products and services. They spearhead change efforts and get them done, while avoiding demoralization and disorganization. They avoid wasted resources, false starts, and failed initiatives and they quickly capitalize on investments in time and resources by making the change processes work.

A senior production manager of a large industrial concern recounts:

> My job is to see that all the pieces of organizational change are done very well. I have to spend a good deal of time *caring* for the change. It's more than caring for people. It means attending to all the details of the whole change process. I have to be completely involved and committed to keep things on track and solve problems.

This manager's viewpoint captures an essential attitude about change leaders. Change leadership is the process of seeing beyond the change goal for hidden barriers and unpredicted consequences of change. Most often, the critical barriers are not technical knowledge or skill. Rather, they are simple oversights, lack of persistence, poor communication, or other more personal vulnerabilities. The ability to overcome the human and organizational barriers to change is the key to innovation. Change leaders do this through their ongoing involvement and monitoring of the process. Most important, they understand that change is a dynamic, evolving set of events that must be managed in a manner similar to other parts of the business.

## WHERE TO START

Leaders understand that change is desirable, but often question why it is so painful and difficult to implement in organizations. One of the primary reasons is that the goals of change are sometimes very nebulous. For example, many CEOs and other senior managers have recently sponsored various projects to change "corporate culture." In part, this may be a result of observing the effect of societal and familial values on the worker's productivity, and the commitment of foreign workers. It is certainly a response to the need for significantly new business attitudes and practices. Although it is critical to business success, changing corporate culture has proven an elusive goal when left as a global concept.

A focus on large, amorphous change often leads to nonspecific interventions, inaction, or frustration. The CEO of a well-known worldwide service company voiced his dilemma:

> I see my principal job as bringing about change in the organization. You know, we have some entrenched opinions around here, but the way we operated in the past isn't good enough for the way we have to operate in the future to be competitive. I know the direction we have to go and, in a way, my job is the easy one—to set the course. But, how can my staff and the organization make the changes I know we have to make?

The most important steps for executing large-scale changes is to make them "smaller." Change leaders answer *specific* organizational needs through *specific* personal behaviors that can be planned and mastered. One change leader stated:

I have to ask myself some hard questions every time I
make a move . . . What concrete, observable outcomes
will result from the change? What specific elements of
the organization need to be changed? Do I want to
have an impact on technological systems, management systems, organizational structures, job designs,
management practices, or some other element of the
organization, or all of these? And, most important,
what should I *say* and *plan* and *do* to make it happen?

For instance, the general manager of a large division of a
Fortune 500 corporation reported:

When I first arrived here, I realized that the business
would have to be shifted radically, if we were ever to
regain market strength again. That meant looking at
our manufacturing methods, our design methods,
our union relations, how we treated our employees,
as well as our whole approach to the customer. I
realized we couldn't change all these overnight, but I
didn't have too much time. The key things we had to
change became *programs*. We had our automated factory program, our integrated design program, our
customer service program, our union relations program. I made it clear that I expected my senior managers to achieve the results we specified each year for
each program. They had several projects in each of
these and *they* made sure these were managed to
achieve concrete results they could see and I could
see!

*Individual leadership skills often determine the success or failure of
an implementation.* One leader made this observation:

When I was put in a leadership role, I wanted to
employ *democratic* practices. I often negated my role
by constantly passing it on to someone else. I thought
this was *delegation*. Mostly, it was just a waste of my

knowledge and influence. As I gained more experience, I realized that delegation is not only assigning tasks, but specifying outcomes and making sure they're met.

This process of *specifying* requires active involvement and the performance of an array of competent behaviors. Often, change leaders must drive the change process by giving specific direction.

Frequently managers will put a great deal of emphasis on the design of a new organization or system. They focus on the overall results and outcomes exclusively. But, it is just as important to focus on the *process* of the dynamics of change. Therefore, change leaders must offer patient, persistent, and consistent guidance.

The senior production manager described the way her new work setting affected the process of change:

I have to be very sensitive to *the various dimensions* of change that are going on here. For one thing, we've merged two different companies. I have a new boss. This, of course, affects me. Now these guys below me are accustomed to a structure where there used to be several layers between them and the executive office. That was enforced in the previous regime. My predecessor liked to maintain an air of regal authority. Suddenly these layers are disappearing. Has their job changed? Not in its fundamentals. But they must be wondering how all this is going to affect them. Now, at the first two levels of the organization, we are changing and clarifying roles. That's a minichange. It seems to be going smoothly. But I also think that it starts to affect these guys who report directly to me. They are squeezed between two changes. In order to maximize the effectiveness of the changes at every level, I have to be sensitive to these dynamics. Any extra element we bring in here has to be brought in with this *context* in mind.

## DEFINE THE CHANGE CONTEXT

Change leaders need to begin with a clear understanding of the effect of change on all aspects of the organization. To define planned change, they must ask:

- What specifically are we changing? And why?
- Where is the starting point?
- Have we charted a reasonable direction?
- What particular part of the organization are we changing or could change as a result of this effort?

*Change leaders focus on the specific context of change.* One manager told us, "There is a real paradox about change. People tend to go to extremes. At first, they have a deep resistance; then when they get going, they tend to go off in unconnected directions and cause as many problems as they solve." The change leader's job is to keep careful control over the process by ensuring that everyone is focused on the same *direction.* However, since the change occurs at several different levels of the organization, it is best to focus on specific domains of organizational activity. But, what are these organizational domains and what are the best ways to maintain focus during planned change?

*The strategic domain* encompasses the overall vision of the total organization. Usually chief executive officers and executive groups concentrate on broad *directions.* Their responsibility is to expand horizons and engender new possibilities. They *point the way,* but avoid defining the steps for reaching these possibilities. They limit their interventions to the larger domain and delegate the details for specifying strategies and carrying out activities to others. Jack Welch, General Electric's CEO, once described the kind of vision needed in the *strategic domain* as a *quantum leap*—a move toward new vistas. He emphasized that the execution of details belonged in other domains.

Change leaders in the *middle of the organization* use the strategic domain as an umbrella for gaining resources. That is why it is so important that someone in a top leadership position set the tone for change. Even in organizations without charismatic or visionary leadership, successful middle-management change leaders must frame their efforts in terms of strategic issues and present change as a means of improving an organization's overall performance.

*The domain of business plans* is the concern of senior or middle management. They are given a vision or focus, such as improving products, services, or processes. This domain provides a bridge between the open-ended challenge of visionaries and the day-to-day actions of employees who must implement detailed objectives. For example, one company executive announced, "We plan to be number one in aerospace in three years. How can we make this happen?" The senior staff was charged with the responsibility of translating this vision into *concrete strategies* that could result in *specific implementation*. The domain of business plans is the area in which change leadership has the most leverage.

*The domain of everyday operations* is executed by first-level or middle management and those to whom top management delegates day-to-day responsibilities. In this domain, leaders frame goals that include deadlines, challenges, obligations, and time frames. This is the arena in which the change leader mobilizes and tracks all resources, including people, until the change project is complete. The primary role of those operating in this domain is to translate strategies into practical objectives.

Once the responsibilities of the domains are clarified, change leaders must translate any change initiative from the level of strategic operations to day-to-day operations. Obviously, this requires an *overall plan* that taps every resource available and utilizes people in the most effective way possible. *Every successful change effort starts with a workable, clearly defined master plan, with specified steps.*

## A FOCUS FOR ACTION

To establish a focus for action, a change leader has to confront three critical problems:

1. *Motivating people to change,*
2. *Obtaining the right resources, and*
3. *Making the change effort workable.*

*Motivating people to change* is one of the major challenges of leadership. People resist change for a variety of reasons. Some people's previous negative experiences teach them that change is hazardous and harmful. Others may not see the rationale for change; they are content with the status quo. Others resist because the reasons for the change are not clearly communicated to them. They have no logical basis for accepting a different way of operating.

The tolerance people have for change is intimately connected to their personalities. People with a high need for basic security often resist making the commitment to change. In contrast, people with a high need to achieve—to do something better, to compete against a standard of excellence—are more likely to embrace change, particularly if they are rewarded during the change effort. They are most responsive if there is a *tangible* payoff for them in the process.

Individuals who work in situations where friendly personal interactions dominate often resist change if they perceive that it threatens these relationships. Similarly, people who seek to influence or control others resist change that interferes with their power and support change if it stabilizes or increases their level of social control.

Perhaps the most essential task of the change leader in motivating and influencing others is *perfecting communication*. Management experts have long extolled the virtues of clear communication. In fact, it was Aristotle who first explored this idea: "Once man *understands* an idea, he can *identify* with it, *acknowledge* it, and *make it his own*." The most effective leaders recognize that the objectives for change must be clearly communicated before the team can *own* them.

*Change leaders also understand that communication requires excellent information.* Exploring ideas is essential for making goals and plans relevant to the end user. The process of inquiry not only generates fruitful information, but also engages participants in a dialogue about change. This avoids externally imposed goals and plans that can never have the full commitment of end users.

Throughout the change process *effective leaders focus on developing the skills of written communication, meeting management, and presentations*. One manager reported:

I couldn't believe we almost blew the plan. We ran a meeting that was so poorly handled that participants assumed our plan was lousy. Fortunately, just before we adjourned, one of our team members quickly sketched our intentions on a flip chart. He saved the day! We had spent an hour confusing the audience and he spent five minutes saving our necks by clarifying the plan. After that the whole group *bought* it with no difficulty.

Motivated implementors are necessary, but not sufficient, to introduce change. In addition, appropriate resources must be mobilized. Although a leader's initiative to *obtain the right resources* requires securing adequate financial backing, its major focus is to secure a team of talented people who can successfully implement the change. One manager described a type of inadequate resources: "This is a great place. They tell us to embrace change. Then I find I have to do everything myself, especially with poor funding and no additional help!" However, not every change requires large scale resources. Michael Cope developed a successful young electronics company in specialized markets by slowly building it through *self-financing*. It was only when he saw that the business had an adequate market that he took *Interphase* public for over four million dollars in cash. The same philosophy applies to internal ventures. Change leaders ensure appropriate resources, on an appropriate scale, at the right time.

*Change leaders foster productive action from their teams.* They structure interventions with skillful goal-setting and use their plan as a *team* contract, a working document to be discussed and modified by team members, but above all, to be implemented. They gather information and opinions from key personnel to increase shared commitment and focus on viable options and opportunities. Team members are assigned specific tasks and "contract" to achieve the organization's goals.

Motivated implementors and working resources supply only the *potential* for change. *Making the change effort workable* is a leader's most crucial responsibility. This requires expert planning and the coordination of each phase during the change process. Some change efforts do not succeed, because leaders fail to connect strategic, business, and everyday plans. Other efforts start with such complicated plans that few people can understand how to proceed on a practical level. Still other changes—with viable and workable plans—provide no training to teach coworkers how to incorporate plans into day-to-day operations or fail to solicit help and information from a wide variety of people who might add substantial support to the change effort.

In our experience, plans that incorporate organizational strategies and functioning have limited impact unless they are rooted in *specific activities* that individuals perform. In other words, a carefully planned process of change serves as an anchor for *goal-directed action*. It helps leaders direct critical initial steps in the change and avoids the overzealous, "get-the-show-on-the-road-at-any-cost" bias of many action-oriented leaders. Sometimes a slower, more methodical approach is better.

In addition to formulating plans carefully, *change leaders help end users visualize specific plan steps* and emphasize how users can improve their own work procedures as well as *achieve their personal goals*. One manager told us:

> When the plan is conceived *only* in someone's mind and not communicated, it is not a *reality*. It is either a figment of someone's imagination or not connected to the needs of users. Only when we effectively communicate the plan can the team become fully motivated or feel any real personal involvement.

*Change leaders know the importance of creating a written, visible plan.* Just as vital, they understand that any written plan must be an outgrowth of a collaborative dialogue with others. Open discussions, interviewing coworkers, and testing the plan with selective workers keep it relevant to end-user needs. Each can play a role in specifying and refining plan steps. Above all, change leaders know that truly innovative plans require many revisions and updates during the change process.

## AVOIDING OVERSIGHTS

Part of change leadership is doing things right; part is avoiding mistakes by ensuring that your organization bypasses the critical traps that undermine planned innovation. Some of the typical oversights include:

1.  *Failure to take end-user needs into account.* The lure of technology often causes people to create elegant systems that do not serve the needs of the people who have to live with them. For example, a manufacturing company had difficulty implementing a sophisticated system for controlling a manufacturing process. The systems designers complained that they did not get very much support from the production people. However, as one foreman stated, "In this job all I need to know is how much we have to produce and where the materials are to do the job. After that, the process takes care of the rest. I don't need fancy computers to keep me up with these things. In fact, they just slow everything down!" A systems analyst later observed, "We had installed a similar system in another plant in the company. I think we did make it a little too complicated for this business and unwittingly invited resistance."

Understanding the needs of the end user is one of the most important keys to overcoming resistance to change. In one successful case we observed, the systems implementors spent a great deal of time on the shop floor talking to operators before introducing a new cutting machine. They understood the operators' existing job from every point of view. They could tell you, with the same understanding as the operators, what they liked and did not like about the cutting operation. As a result, they were able to set up the system in a way that helped the operators, (as well as the foreman and plant management), to eliminate some of the frustrations in their jobs.

2.  *Failure to recognize all of the functions (roles) involved in the change.* Change projects depend on a mix of people and skills for success. Some project teams have members with tremendous technical talent, but fail because they lack someone with people skills. Others fail from a deficit of technical expertise. Learning how to balance the various demands of planned change is a key leadership skill. In all cases several roles must work in concert. The leader who can coordinate different, often conflicting, viewpoints is just as necessary as the committed leader who develops and sells the program. As one implementor related, "I spend about 60 percent of my time

dealing with anxious people. Most of what I do is calming people down and keeping my management colleagues on board about what we are doing."

3. *Failure to delegate responsibilities.* Many change leaders, particularly those from technical backgrounds, tend to become too involved with the steps of implementation at some stages of the change process. Successful projects involve many people, each one playing a complementary role. Choosing the most appropriate role for oneself is a key issue in any change effort. One CEO told us, "I decided that in order to transform my organization, I needed to spearhead our relationships with the outside world. I got things going at the highest levels in our customers' organizations. That's my strength. I found others who could focus that same level of energy on internal matters." Successful change leaders accurately assess their strengths and weaknesses, delegating the tasks for which they are less suited to coworkers.

4. *Failure to recognize who will be affected by change.* When a supplier of industrial commodities centralized its order entry system, executives felt they could generate more profits by having fewer people in their regions and maintaining more control over prices. Within weeks, the complaints mounted from those accustomed to calling up their local office. Over a period of years, they had developed some shorthand methods for ordering the product. These were particular to each region and to certain customers. Unfortunately, the shorthand expressions did not correspond to the order entry codes on the new system. Therefore, the customer was presented with a significant barrier to placing new orders. "I guess we blew it," said the vice-president for sales. "We spent a lot of time telling the sales force how the new system worked. We sent an explanation to the customer. The missing link was: we just hadn't listened to find out *how* some of our largest customers ordered!"

Successful change leaders ask about the consequences of change on those affected. From many perspectives, they focus on the problems the change is designed to solve. In addition, they test the feasibility of various ideas with end users. Most important, they keep communicating with all affected individuals throughout the change effort.

5. *Failure to develop an influence strategy to get support for change.* Some leaders believe the rationale for change is so compelling that they never have to justify it to anyone else. People have a variety of interests and motivations. Therefore, time has to be spent developing support at all levels of the organization. Having top management support without the support of people below means that the project will probably succeed, but only after delays from resistance. Support from below, but with no support from top management usually spells the death of a project from limited resources.

Obtaining support for change is more than merely communicating its purpose. Effective change leaders think about who will be affected, whose support is necessary, and consciously adopt strategies to ensure that they obtain this support.

6. *The tendency to consider only short-term costs.* This oversight is especially typical of large organizations that put a heavy weight on accounting for returns on investment. Obviously, it is essential to account rigorously for a change project. However, a change project is only part of a stream of other activities that are happening in an organization. Some organizations push through change as if there were no tomorrows. This has long-term costs, some of which are tangible, others more elusive, even psychological in nature.

Effective change leaders think through the long-term consequences of change and weigh the costs and benefits of specific actions. A CEO recounted:

> We wanted a more radical organizational design, but I realized that to do that, we would have to go outside of the organization for an implementation team. I think that we could have achieved some quick results and a number of my senior managers wanted me to do that, but I believed in my own people. So, I saw the small changes we were making, more slowly, as an investment in the future."

7. *The tendency not to define expectations clearly.* Systems may eventually get implemented. Most organizations survive new organizational designs. However, lack of clarity about what to expect in the change effort is a prime cause of resistance to change. When a company put in a system to track the time staff people were spending on various projects, the management thought it a rather innocuous system. After all, at the end of each day, all the workers had to do was enter on a rather friendly screen what they had worked on for that day. The management staff saw this as an efficient way of accounting for time. They felt they could make better estimates to their clients as to how long it would take to deliver some jobs. They also planned to introduce a system of "billing" in the operations. However, these intentions were never clearly communicated to the workers. As one manager put it, "We spent a lot of time making sure people could use the system. I'm sure we told them *why* we were introducing the system, but somehow that got lost." It was only after the system had obviously stopped being used that managers discovered that workers thought that the system had been designed to help rationalize reducing the number of positions in the department.

An accurate test for whether expectations are defined correctly is asking people at different levels of an organization about a change effort. If leaders obtain the same answer from all those questioned, then they can be assured expectations are defined correctly. Effective change leaders ensure that expectations are communicated and are consistent across the entire organization.

8. *The tendency to ignore complaints instead of considering their possible legitimacy.* A number of managers will tell you that "people are never satisfied" or that "no one likes to change." Therefore you should expect complaints and charge ahead anyway. However, successful leaders use complaints as a source of information about how to improve a change effort. It is true that not everyone can be satisfied with every effort, but ignoring complaints may cause a leader to overlook a valuable piece of information. As one worker told us:

I told them that having to go down to the central tool room for my special tools instead of having them on the floor with me was wasting time. A year later they bring in this consultant and he does a study. Lo and behold, he tells them it's a waste of time for me to have to walk to central tools every time I need to use the special tools. He shows them figures about how it would be more efficient to equip all riggers with special tools instead of sharing them centrally. Didn't I tell everybody that a year ago? I may not be a Harvard MBA, but I do have common sense!

The worker's manager later admitted that it would have been profitable to talk to him before hiring a consultant. Effective change leaders see complaints as related to information they can use to ensure the clarity of communications, expectations, influence strategies and roles. As one systems implementor reported, "I much prefer vocal critics to silent resisters. I can sit down with my outspoken critics and do something about what they say. But I can't beat silence."

Obviously change leaders grant that all of the suggestions just described to combat failure are desirable and necessary—very much as good parents agree they must be attentive, fair, caring, and alert to their children's needs—but in today's fast-moving business arena, they look for a practical, down-to-earth method for carrying out the responsibility. As we move to the next chapters, you will learn how to assess an organization's strengths and vulnerabilities around change. We provide simple strategies for correcting weaknesses that can interfere with, or altogether prohibit, effective change. At the same time, you will learn how to capitalize on your organization's strengths.

The *actions* of best leaders effect innovations by preparing their organizations for change, assigning specific people to responsibilities and holding them accountable for them, creating plans with specific milestones and deadlines, and directing a successful implementation.

## MAKE IT PERSONAL

1. Think of a significant planned change effort in which you have been involved and in what domain you were operating.
   • The strategic domain?
   • The business plan domain?
   • The everyday operations domain?

2. What were some of the strategies you used to prevent chaos?

3. To define the planned change, did you ask:
   • What specifically are we changing? And why?
   • Where is the starting point?
   • Have we charted a reasonable direction?
   • What particular aspect (domain) of the organization are we changing or could we change as a result of this effort?

4. What were the biggest motivational problems in the effort?

5. How were resources obtained for the effort? Include a description of how you formed your change team.

6. Did the change effort fall into any of these traps?
   - Failure to take end-user needs into account?
   - Failure to recognize all of the functions (roles) involved in change?
   - Failure to delegate responsibilities?
   - Failure to recognize who will be affected?
   - Failure to develop an influence strategy to get support for the change?
   - Tendency to consider only short-term costs?
   - Tendency not to define expectations clearly?
   - Tendency to ignore complaints instead of considering their possible legitimacy?

# PART II

# A MODEL OF
# BEST PRACTICES
# FOR PLANNED
# CHANGE

# CHAPTER 4

# Getting Ready for Change

*Upfront preparation that increases the fit between
a change and organizational practices and values
is the necessary foundation for planned
innovation.*

ARMORTECH: THE ROBOTS ARE COMING!
Carl Tomassi was upset. Sam Redstone, sent from
headquarters to introduce robots to Tomassi's plant,
was his target. "Look, you come here and tell me you
want a robot to do the work of my employees. You'll
make all the plans, take care of everything. But the
bottom line is that I'll be taking all the risks. If the
thing flops, it'll be my loss. Why should I stick out my
neck that far?"

Redstone was prepared for resistance, particularly
since Tomassi hadn't been included in the decision.
But he was surprised by the intensity of Tomassi's
outburst. In Redstone's brief tenure at Armortech
Corporation, a division of a multinational corporation that fabricates heavy metals for various indus-

tries, he had been part of several successful projects to upgrade engineering practices. The president, Mark Waterfield, was a shoot-from-the-hip type of guy, committed to pushing his "smokestack" business into a high-tech world—maybe a little too committed and a little too fast to keep people informed about his plans. But Waterfield had strengths too. He was decisive and charismatic. After viewing a film on robotics, he decided this was a critical step toward profits and productivity.

Redstone got his new assignment in typical Waterfield fashion—quick and to the point.

"Robots!" Waterfield said, as he greeted Redstone in the lunch line.

"What?" Redstone replied hesitantly, as he asked for a tuna on rye.

"We've got to shape up and fast. We can't just do a good job and expect profits. We need a 'home run'—a major leap in productivity. Bionic clean-up hitters—robots!" Waterfield exclaimed.

Redstone was about to ask a question. Waterfield continued as he bubbled with enthusiasm, "I've heard great things about you and I want you to make it happen. Remember, home runs, not base hits."

Then he walked away.

An engineer by training, Redstone was eager for the assignment. But after quickly researching the problem, he was uneasy about the lack of specific guidance from the top. In fact, he regretted not asking all those questions he had for Waterfield.

After searching for a division to begin the project, he settled on Carl Tomassi's plant in Alabama. Redstone made his pick based on two factors: the plant was located in a rural area, so any initial problems would have less exposure; and it was not unionized, so there would be less resistance to innovation.

Carl Tomassi's resistance to robots was understandable. If the project succeeded he wouldn't get credit; if it failed, he'd probably get the blame. Redstone knew he needed to give Tomassi realistic support.

"I'll pay for the implementation and take full public responsibility for the project. You'll get final say about any plans," Redstone offered. Tomassi complied, providing Redstone with a desk, office space, and access to records, the work area, and people in various departments.

Redstone was pleased with his progress until he found even stronger opposition to the change from the technical staff in the plant. One of them said, "You guys just want to put people out of work to save money. Besides, I don't think it'll work; we've got some very technical work that requires last minute changes. I'd like to see a machine do that!"

Redstone listened to complaints and didn't argue. He knew he needed to do something quick and visible to allay fears. While touring the plant, he looked for a place that a robot might make a big initial impression. His own discomfort watching the furnace work gave him his answer. The operator took parts from a bin on his left, inserted them in a carousel in the furnace, in front of him, then removed the molten material and placed it in a press to his right. The carousel moved every 15 seconds, requiring a new part with every turn. The worker was in constant motion.

Sweat dripped continuously from the operator's brow, as he responded in a monotone to Redstone's question about his daily quota, "1,050 pieces every single day! But, at least I get paid a good hourly wage."

Redstone inquired further, "How do you really like your work?"

The worker hesitated and then said, "Well, I get by . . . it's honest, hard work."

Redstone knew where to start the implementation and he knew he needed help. The factory wasn't his turf. With Tomassi's advice, he formed a team with members from different groups—manufacturing, quality control, maintenance, shop operations, and employee relations. Mostly he tried to get wide representation of individuals he thought could influence their peers.

Unfortunately, rumors spread faster than one person can work. By this time, *robot* had become a dirty word—a kind of symbol of management power and control. But nobody had even seen a robot in action! So, Redstone gave a brief presentation. He showed the film that impressed the president and illustrated specific ways that robots can help. The team responded positively enough to gain a consensus about using a robot for the furnace work. Redstone knew he'd turned a corner when a member said, "I'm sold. It's a solid idea. We upgrade a boring and dangerous job and robots don't even sweat or call in sick."

As team planning meetings continued over the subsequent weeks, members began to talk about implementation in *we* terms. This helped when a final wave of resistance emerged. There was talk on the floor and throughout the plant about robots taking away jobs. Rumors escalated about layoffs, demotions, and insensitive management. A personnel representative even set up an emergency meeting with Redstone, Tomassi, and the implementation team.

Tomassi was on the spot. He'd allowed plans to proceed, but hadn't been very involved or supportive. Redstone was on the spot too. He'd unintentionally alienated the work force and was still an outsider to most people. After hearing about the problem, Tomassi asked for suggestions to stem the rumors. The team was ready. They assured Tomassi the project would work if there was a clear policy on layoffs. Together, the team, Tomassi, and Redstone forged a three-part policy:

1. No workers would lose their jobs because of the introduction of robots; jobs would only be lost through attrition.
2. Plans for wider use of robots would proceed only after the success of the prototype.
3. Robotics would then proceed in planned *phases.*

The first robot was introduced to the plant furnace work area during an off-shift. A large crowd of workers had gathered to watch. Redstone, like an expectant father, watched nervously as the switch was pulled and the robot swung into action. It worked! In fact, it was mesmerizing. Workers applauded, team members congratulated each other.

Redstone turned to Tomassi, "No sweat, heh."

Tomassi nodded his head, winked, and said, "No sick days either."

Seeing the robot in action relieved most of the workers' imagined fears. They even made suggestions about how to improve its efficiency. As a result, the robot quickly exceeded the production quota and became one of the work force.

The most significant change came over Tomassi. Once he saw how successful the robot was, he was a convert—a real robot zealot.

At Armortech implementors did some things well and many things poorly. Hard work, personal tolerance, and a little luck saw them through. However, in the rush to modernize, each person in the chain of command failed to create an environment for confronting the cultural impediments to change. In particular, the president worked under the assumption that large-scale cultural change would occur as a result of his mandate. He and his subordinates overlooked the need for translating visions at the *macro* level to goals and tasks that affect *micro* operations. *Fitting the change to the context* in which change occurs is a critical, frequently ignored, necessity for success.

Armortech is a typical "smokestack" corporation with all the basic problems facing today's industrial companies—aging factories and machinery, multiple layers of management, unused manufacturing capacity, and a culture that sustains inefficient policies and practices. The maladies of our industrial arena have been a major concern for the past several years. However, similar problems from worldwide competition are starting to emerge in various service industries. Already we are seeing significant change initiatives in financial services and insurance companies as a result of strong competitive pressures. The problems with preparing for a technological change in manufacturing, such as robotics, will apply increasingly to the service sector as well.

However, even as the need for change has become more evident, some leaders fear innovation, clinging tightly to traditional controls and the status quo. Others eagerly pursue change for change's sake—often running headlong into unseen stumbling blocks.

Every business develops a working environment that influences all work practices and employees. From the minute-to-minute influences on productivity represented by "human ergonomic" factors, such as lighting, furniture design, or a unique environment, to the forces inherent in organizational values, each setting is a complex set of factors that can enhance or impede change. Labeled *culture,* these attributes provide enough stability to produce organized work practices and output, and yet they frequently suppress new ideas and interfere with adaptive responses to a changing world. For example, most large corporations have built headquarters that present an image of success and solidity. At one of America's largest companies, serenity and clean elegance emanate from a few simple low-lying buildings surrounded by maples blanketing the rolling hills of southern Connecticut. Although the view from corporate headquarters looks like an ad for a New England country inn, the buildings are hard-edged corporate reality. The surroundings reinforce a definite mind-set—calm, yet organized and focused—a rolling landscape, waterfalls, sprawling rhododendrons on the outside; on the inside, deep carpeted corridors in lush color schemes lined with original art. These contrast with an open office environment with islands of clean desks and clusters of computer terminals and printers, duplicators, and fax machines. The setting seems to say, "We'll take care of you, but we expect hard work."

In contrast, a group from a large clothing retailer recently moved from its lush corporate headquarters to a cramped warehouse, feeling that the elegant surroundings had lulled them into complacency and softness. They envisioned, in a more austere environment, forming a small group of warriors hardened to battle for their market share of the designer apparel market. Instead, they got a demoralized, insecure, less creative, less productive team of workers.

Successful change leaders know they have to pay attention to the context into which they introduce change efforts. Organizations that prepare carefully for change by considering factors related to their culture can often start a positive feedback loop for change. In other words, tailoring the change to the context always makes it a more successful enterprise. In turn, this favorable result becomes part of the context for all future change efforts, making them more likely to succeed, too.

## IS THE ORGANIZATION READY FOR CHANGE?

To start the change process more effectively, this chapter focuses on a simple, tested, step-by-step method for preparing managers and their coworkers. Looking at an organization's readiness to change is the first step in discovering barriers to planned innovation and developing effective strategies for change across five dimensions. When introducing change, we particularly look at critical factors in an organization's culture. Failing to recognize the importance of each of these factors can impede a change effort. As we outlined in Chapter 2, the factors essential for preparing an organization are:

- The History of Change,
- The Clarity of Expectations,
- The Origin of the Problem or Idea,
- The Amount of Top Management Support, and
- The Compatibility of the Change with Other Aspects of the Organization.

In the ensuing pages, we will define these attributes and focus on how the best leaders build strategies around these critical areas of an organization's culture.

## THE BEST PREDICTOR OF FUTURE SUCCESS IS PAST HISTORY!

At Armortech, Sam Redstone eventually produced positive results, but he took some large and unnecessary chances by not learning much more about his company's *history of change* experiences.

One of the most reliable tenets about planned change is

hackneyed, but true: "success breeds success." Those who are successful at change efforts tend to have been successful before. This can be somewhat disheartening to potential change leaders in an organization with a poor record of effectively making changes. It is not inevitable that these leaders have to be discouraged! They just have to work harder at developing strategies for overcoming their organization's vulnerabilities.

The first step is to *gather information* about previous successes and failures. It is important not to short-change information-gathering. This process helps uncover the critical barriers to planned innovation, and it gives coworkers a chance to ask questions and develop ownership of a project. In simplest terms, the greater the past resistance to change, the greater the need in the present for informal and formal discussions about problems and plans. *Most problems can be overcome by spending extra time talking.*

*Extra time talking often can also allay fears about change.* An executive of a national grocery chain knew "extra talking" and exploring might help his coworkers adopt a new idea. He proposed that the addition of lunch bars in the stores could be profitable. But he learned this same idea had been turned down three years previously. However, in reviewing the history of this rejection, he discovered that the person introducing the idea had tried to *railroad it through.* He decided to begin slow and easy. At a meeting, he proposed:

> Some of us on the executive board have come up with an idea that we think will work, but as I share it with you, I want to assure you that we expect to explore it with caution. The idea is to investigate the possibility of all stores having lunch bars. . . . Consumers immediately get hungry when they walk in and see the food displays . . . why not feed them? And for them, it is a one-stop time saver—load up on groceries for home and pick up a fast bite to eat at the same time. (Besides, it might help stop all of the pilfering and tasting fruit in produce and nibbling on cookies in the cookie bins.) . . . Now because it's an new idea for us, I suggest we spend an entire day sorting out the pros and cons. First, we have to explore what the change

can mean. I am appointing a task force to spend two weeks *gathering information*. Then, we can have an all-day meeting to devote plenty of time to *talking through* all of the possibilities.

This executive did several things right. He did not push the idea through without giving his coworkers time to explore the possibilities and problems. He put emphasis on information-gathering by appointing an able task force and he arranged an entire day in the work schedule to *spend extra time talking*. Most of all, the leader laid an appropriate foundation for change.

The companion skill to information-gathering is *providing appropriate, ongoing feedback*. Redstone actually provoked some of the most negative reactions to change. For example, if he had made information about change plans available and if he had explained each step in his implementation well *before* it happened, most rumors and distortions could have been avoided. Unfortunately, leaders often act on their instincts without vital information, particularly when they anticipate conflicts or delays in implementation. This approach is short-sighted and unfair to coworkers. Managers are deprived of critical feedback and workers feel no ownership of ongoing policies and practices.

Redstone did many things with considerable skill. He built a support team and a network to uphold his efforts. He also provided enough technical information about robotics to make a good case for change. However, he was also the emissary of Waterfield's action-oriented bias and in a hurry. By not explaining the need for robotics in the framework of a competitive environment, Redstone failed to communicate a compelling reason for greater efficiency—a viable business!

Group resistance to change often remains hidden until critical steps in the planned innovation must be implemented. By involving participants *prior* to specific changes in policies or practices, a leader can often confront deep-seated, negative attitudes before they become barriers. After a study identified significant skill deficits in supervisors, leaders at a retail company decided to implement a management development program. The findings were distributed and discussed with supervisors, who then *asked for* a skill development program. Top management avoided having to mandate solutions by helping supervisors develop their own prescription for the management deficit.

*Change leaders arrange for a quick payoff to overcome historical resistance.* In this way, members of the organization can see that the change results in *direct* and *immediate* benefits for them.

### A VISIBLE PAYOFF

In a project aimed at increasing material handling efficiency on a large corporation's loading dock, change implementors used two effective strategies. They chose a receptive group of workers and they introduced change in small steps. Management selected crane operators, not dock workers, to computerize material-handling. The crane operators were young, free spirits, with a visible presence in the factory. For several weeks, the drivers drove around using new, hand-held microprocessors to track parts. Slowly, word spread through the factory grapevine. Workers on the loading dock actually began to request the new devices from management for themselves. By starting the change with a group of workers that ensured a quick, positive, visible payoff, the company overcame the dock workers' resistance to new practices.

Change is always a stressful enterprise, partly because organizations are comprised of workers with different attitudes and tolerances for new ideas. To overcome initial resistance, the effective leader makes the first aspects of implementation *small, simple,* and *selective.* A large international bank with a conservative culture started its new computerized banking system at a branch run by a highly innovative manager. The potential for computerizing a wide range of bank transactions was presented at first, but not implemented. Instead, new work routines were initially limited to transactions requiring a few keystrokes compatible with usual operations. Moving more slowly resulted in a more comfortable, uniformly positive response to the new system. The staff began to request additional functions; and as word of success spread through the organization, other branch managers wanted to use the system. In this case, slower was faster.

Sometimes organizational culture, anchored in myths and group norms, undermines change. Often, the inherent tensions between management and employees impede innovative efforts. Frequently, so-called "sociotechnical" conflicts between working relationships and the operational aspects of a business mediate against change. And almost always, people individually and collectively resist the anxiety and uncertainty that change inevitably produces.

There is often a gap between "pie in the sky" pronouncements, managerial homilies, or panaceas and workaday demands. Compliance with either pole inhibits productive change. Ultimately, organizations adapt when cultural forces and upper management visions are translated into practical, personal strategies and goals that provide a path to new work practices.

Since each organization has its own culture and each part of an organization its own unique group processes, the wise manager facilitates change by confronting vulnerabilities produced by past experiences with innovation.

**To summarize:**

---

If History of Change is a barrier to change:
- Explain change plans fully.
- Skillfully present plans.
- Make information readily available.
- Make sure plans include benefits for end users and for the corporation.
- Spend extra time talking.
- Ask for additional feedback from the work force.
- Start small and simple.
- Arrange for a quick, positive, visible payoff.
- Publicize successes.

---

## WHAT YOU EXPECT MAY NOT BE WHAT YOU GET

Every change leader must deal with expectations. In fact, *clarity of expectations* about change is one of the most critical issues in planned innovation. One way to assess the "clarity of expectations" in an organization is to ask senior managers to explain what the change is going to accomplish; then ask people further down the organization the same question. If both groups offer the same explanation, the organization probably has a fairly uniform set of expectations that have been communicated either directly or indirectly.

But what do leaders do if various members of the organization have different viewpoints about the impact of change? How do they prevent end users from becoming confused or misinformed? What should they do to specify changed goals?

At Armortech, people had an array of very personal concerns and hopes about what the introduction of robots would mean. For President Waterfield, it meant higher profit margins and a modern image. For Carl Tomassi, it was mostly a loss of control. For other plant management, change was more work. For Redstone, it was a challenge. Finally, for the workers, it was a threat to their jobs.

*Change leaders define and emphasize common interests to overcome different perspectives.* Somehow Redstone needed to formulate a plan for change that emphasized its benefits for end users and its relationship to the overall corporate mission. By focusing on the common benefits for all participants, he could have prevented much of the ensuing friction.

### GOOD FOR YOU AND US

A large computer firm was introducing one of a series of new products. The president held several meetings to emphasize the strategic importance of better communications to match new product introductions. However, he noted openly the problems change had caused in hiring and retaining quality staff over the last five years. The president emphasized that the engineering personnel felt disempowered and lacking in vital information about new directions. He pointed out the need for increased support of the marketing and sales staff in the field.

The president even read from a plaintive letter he had received: "I'm confused and demoralized. My quota goes up every year no matter what. But, we have more than a hundred products. Which should I push the most? Which ones represent our future directions? What can I tell customers about exactly when we plan to meet their needs?"

After focusing on the problem, the president introduced plans for an information center—a clearinghouse for product support, product development information, as well as questions from employees. This plan found wide acceptance, since it encompassed common benefits for individuals while it furthered the overall corporate objective.

*Change leaders take into account the different viewpoints of various work groups in a simple, clear manner.* All assumptions about the impact of the change and all expected outcomes should be specified in detail. After taking an inventory of opinions and concerns, successful leaders tell the work force up front about expected problems and expected results. At Armortech, Redstone failed to clarify the assumptions behind the change he was asked to introduce. Furthermore, he never really developed clear outcomes. Without a clear rationale and specific goals, the change became a threat rather than a strategic necessity.

It is not enough to be open with information about the change. Skillful leaders also ensure an ongoing two-way communication process. Depending on the organization's culture, leaders can plan intermittent communication sessions, poll workers, and clarify suggestions and concerns in informal discussions. Remember that these interactions must include *give-and-take dialogue* in which free expression—even sharply critical opinions—is nurtured. In fact, impediments to change often can be reframed as the critical challenges that must be confronted to ensure successful implementation.

A senior manager at a large company undertaking a very extensive organizational restructuring tried to push his program through without a preliminary dialgoue. People complained that they did not know how they would fit into the new organization. He recounted how he really could not be open with information or expect to use everybody's feedback:

> There are over four thousand people involved and a good percentage of them will not be working for us in the new organization. There are incredible political issues between the leaders of the divisions involved. We have to announce the new organization within a certain time frame, because we face significant external pressures, particularly in the stock market. We just have to stick it out and deal with each issue as it comes up.

In retrospect, the executive regretted his urgency. Because he lost more than six months of productive operations and created an ongoing climate of distrust. This was an expensive approach for something designed to reduce costs! By clarifying expectations—particularly initial outcomes and where each person would fit into the new organization—he could have generated support rather than resistance. If leaders cannot make commitments about expected outcomes, then they must specify the process by which they are going to match people to the new organizational requirements.

**To summarize:**

---

If *Clarity of Expectations* is a barrier to change:
- Emphasize the common interests of all participants.
- Specify all assumptions about the impact of the change, including potential problems.
- Communicate plans clearly.
- Ask for feedback.
- Don't suppress negative opinions.
- Focus on clear outcomes.

---

## WHOSE IDEA WAS THIS ANYWAY?

Every change leader should understand how the *origin of an idea or problem* affects the implementation process. A basic axiom of any change effort is that "the further away the people defining the change are from the people who have to live with the change, then the more likelihood that the change will develop problems." At Armortech, Redstone perhaps faced his biggest challenge in bridging the distance between an ill-defined edict from President Waterfield and the daily routines of hourly workers in Alabama. In fact, workers did not perceive their procedures as a problem. For example, the furnace worker did not *request* robotics as an aid for increased efficiency. Although he admitted that his job was hard, he said he was paid well and seemed satisfied. In any case, when the impetus for change does not emanate from the end user, the reasons for the change must be translated into a set of terms and practices that make sense to them. This increases the likelihood of their accepting the change.

For example, two factories in the same part of the country were producing fairly similar products. Both were trying to introduce computer-aided numerical control equipment. In one, where there was a pressing need to replace a cutting machine, the manufacturing engineers took the opportunity to persuade the plant manager that his current method of controlling the machine—using paper tape—was old-fashioned. At the second plant, the manufacturing technologists observed the operators in action. They talked about their problems. They discussed the shop-floor manager's difficulties in detail with him. It was clear that everybody in the plant hated paper tape, because it broke frequently, resulting in wasted materials.

The first site ran into tremendous difficulties during implementation. When they faced technical difficulties, the plant manager became enraged. They even had to lease a tape-driven numerical control machine temporarily to placate him and help make his scheduled requirements. At the second plant everybody enthusiastically embraced the new system. Even when it ran into trouble, the supervisor and his operators worked to resolve problems. They now have a fabrication unit running totally by computer-driven numerical control. Their counterparts, not so far away, are still "temporarily" leasing a tape-driven machine.

At Armortech, Redstone should have started with an open mind and open ears to workers' concerns and suggestions. He could have done this in a variety of ways—a presentation and discussion, a brainstorming session, or a survey regarding attitudes toward potential effects from robotics. Each method would have encouraged an open dialogue and provided vital information for more efficient implementation. By not setting up a collaborative process, Redstone fostered several "us-against-them" struggles.

Besides defining barriers to innovations, *the best change agents make a case for change.* Leaders should specify up front who wants the change and why. They must explain the advantages of the change for the organization in a way that highlights the common benefits for the work force. For example, one major manufacturing firm found little resistance to a management reorganization when coworkers were presented with the company's choice: a radical decrease in layers of personnel—or bankruptcy. In this case it was important for leadership to present, clearly and completely, the potential problems for end users. When the communication gap between top management and the work force is particularly large, a leader should invoke special measures for developing common goals, including: (1) a formal, polished presentation about the change; (2) a clear, public statement about the organization's direction and a rationale for it; and (3) a framework for direct dialogue between top management and others, such as *skip-level* meetings.

*Change leaders take time to talk.* Engendering an open dialogue is usually not enough. For large changes or planned innovations that produce significant organizational conflict, change leaders need to spend extra time listening to problems, providing information, and establishing allies, networks, and support groups. Redstone's use of these strategies was the key to his success and gave him strong formal support in his conflict with Carl Tomassi over job layoffs and vital informal support throughout Armortech.

*Change leaders consider end-user needs first whenever possible.* This entails finding terms and goals resonant with their concerns. For example, in many organizational cultures, the work force has adopted robotics as a way to "become competitive," to "gain new job skills," to increase "quality or excellence" of work output. In addition, skillful leaders arrange for quick, visible, positive outcomes. They then use feedback about the level of stress or concern engendered by the change as a barometer for determining the rate at which to introduce subsequent phases of implementation. For example, a large legal firm arranged for a successful introduction of individual computer work stations by starting the process with a small group of secretaries who put together case material and did word processing. They not only got quick, personally rewarding results, but also advertised the increased productivity of work stations through the increased volume and quality of the documents they generated.

**To summarize:**

---

If the *Origin of the Idea or Problem* is a barrier to change:
- Specify and confront end-user concerns first.
- Clarify who wants the change and why.
- Present a clear case for change.
- Bridge the communication gaps among various groups in the organization.
- Spend more time communicating.
- Set goals that address end users' concerns first.
- Arrange for a quick, visible payoff.

---

## TOP-DOWN SUPPORT

Successful change is closely linked to the amount of *support from top management.* At Armortech, Sam Redstone was given complete responsibility to implement the change, but received little help from the top management. He was given no resources besides money, no formal structure to get feedback from top management during the course of the project, and no clear guidance about exactly why robotics was an important strategy. Many of these deficits would have been overcome if Redstone had followed a few simple guidelines to build support and gather resources for change.

Resources are the raw energy of change; they come in various forms: information, individual skills, relationships, group myths and values, materials, or fiscal support. Some of these assets must be developed informally by all change leaders. Many require the blessing of top management, if not the direct support. To maximize success, the effective change leader must first build a power base by developing allies, selling the change as a compelling need, and mastering knowledge pertinent to the proposed innovation.

A young manager at a financial services corporation envisioned significantly greater security and savings in labor costs and losses through theft by designing a credit card with an embedded computer chip that could automatically provide credit information and unique identifying data, such as an individual's phone number or address. Since the initial investment was substantial, top executives were cool to the idea at first. Their reticence decreased only after the manager convinced a vice-president about her idea on a plane trip and enlisted the support of two computer specialists from a prestigious university to provide technical backup support and endorsement.

Too often change leaders "prime the pump," but fail to get a broad enough consensus for success. In any organization, a natural balance exists between the impetus to change and the tendency to resist new ideas. Therefore, individuals who initiate change must also sustain it. When top management support is weak or inconsistent, this is done best by developing a management review process that includes a formal review with a clear agenda; participation by upper-level personnel; avoiding adversarial roles by asking for specific help; and focusing on practical outcomes, such as goals, milestones, resources, or personnel.

The initiative for fulfilling these criteria can come from a project leader or from top management itself. At Armortech, Redstone probably would have garnered Tomassi's support and avoided much of the resistance to change by sustaining a formal dialogue at a top management level.

**To summarize:**

---

If lack of *Top Management Support* is a barrier to change:
- Become knowledgeable about the change.
- Develop upper-level allies.
- Develop informal coalitions for support.
- Build a case for change that appeals to top-level concerns.
- Start and sustain a formal management review process.
- Ask for help.
- Keep focused on practical outcomes.

---

## WE'RE SO COMPATIBLE

Every leader who initiates a policy, program, or practice should assess the *compatibility of the change* with the current organizational culture:

- Does the change fit with an overall business plan?
- Do proposed changes make employees' jobs harder or easier?
- Is the change technically familiar to members of the organization?

Every competent leader knows the value of communication, but there is never enough for everybody! Successful change leaders overcome this deficit by linking change to other elements of people's jobs and organizational setting. They "piggy back" communications about the change onto already existing channels.

In Waterfield's organization there were no clearly defined business goals that robotics fulfilled, and there were no initial benefits presented to workers. Only much later in the change process did either strategies or front-line advantages become evident—and then only in the context of the robotics film. By then Redstone had already unwittingly fostered fantasies about robots and distrust of management. Instead, he could have publicized general organizational goals and specified in clear, simple terms how a proposed change plan fit with them. In addition, he could have outlined plans that incorporated organizational values and practices and clarified practical benefits to end users. Redstone's lack of information-gathering at the beginning of his assignment did not serve him well. Although no explicit organizational goals, other than increasing productivity, were announced, there were numerous other implicit goals that were part of the company's culture. Redstone should have gotten some consensus about goals and directions before initiating any plans—perhaps even prior to contacting Tomassi.

When a planned change is carefully linked to organizational values and goals, even a hard-to-accept policy can often be introduced without major resistance. A food processor introduced a new manufacturing line in an incredibly fast time span. Management felt that speed was necessary in order to meet a competitive challenge from another company. They communicated this concern to their workers, but challenged them to make the new product meet or surpass their standards for highest quality. Supervisors and workers willingly worked around the clock to put in the new line.

Most organizations have a variety of work settings and group processes. Often a change leader can select an environment with flexible or knowledgeable workers, innovative or skillful managers, or strong advocates. At one teaching hospital, a new type of nursing care was started with a ward staff comprised mostly of new graduates eager for fresh ideas and challenges.

Although an optimistic, energetic approach is most helpful, a leader should not oversell change. It is always stressful and often introduces substantive conflicts and hardships. Effective leaders allow end users to see exactly what is involved in a change effort. For example, an insurance company was introducing automation in their claims division. Many workers feared the increased use of computer terminals. Rather than dismissing their fears, managers took them to see similar systems in operations and let them talk to other workers who had gone through the transition. Based on their newly acquired research, clerks even formed their own task force to implement the change.

**To summarize:**

---

If *Compatibility of Change* is a barrier:
- Specify how the change fits with overall organizational directions.
- Make plans overt, concrete, simple.
- Integrate the change into ongoing procedures whenever possible.
- Initially implement the change in the most accepting surroundings.
- Don't oversell the change.

---

Top performing organizations develop an ethic that supports success. They grow and adapt by promoting change as a value throughout the work force. By making sure significant changes fit with the culture and history of the organization, leaders lay the groundwork for the remainder of the change process.

## MAKE IT PERSONAL

Often change leaders fail to confront the hidden, yet substantive barriers, posed by the organizational environment. By developing effective strategies along the *five dimensions of organizational readiness*, a change leader can:

- Clarify expectations about the change,
- Gain commitment for support both from end users and top management, and
- Frame the change to fit with overall organizational practices and goals.

To determine if your organization is ready for change along the five dimensions of organizational readiness, answer the following questions about a potential change or one in progress:

1.  Is it clear who wants the change and why?

2.  Are plans for change and its outcomes explained in a simple, detailed way?

3.  Are plans for change put in terms that are meaningful to those who must live with them?

4.  Are the common benefits for the organization and workers clear?

5.  Is there strong support for change from top management?

6.  Are potential problems or conflicts with present practices stated up front?

7.  Do you or your management spend enough time gathering information and opinions, defining potential problems, and getting feedback about the changes?

8.  Do you or your management build enough support for change (e.g., teams, coalitions, advocates, supporters)?

9.  Do you initially introduce change in a small, accepting part of the organization?

10. Does your change plan confront the problems of those who will be most affected?

11. Do you reward individual participation in the change process and publicize successes?

# CHAPTER 5

# Getting the Right People

*Planned change relies on getting the right people with the right attributes into the right role at the right time.*

## BEST INTENTIONS

It had been three months since the new phone system had been installed. Frank, president of a rapidly expanding engineering consulting firm of about 60 employees, was pouring over some papers as Sam, his comptroller, came sprinting into his office. "I've got Bill on the line . . . That's the NBE Corporation call you've been expecting. He's got to talk with you now; he wants to give us the contract, but I can't get the damn phone to transfer any place but the Twilight Zone."

Frank—calm, decisive, organized, and confident, as usual—pulled out his information card and piped up, "OK, you just click the button once, dial my extension—201—and when I answer, just hang up."

Sam turned on his heels and sped off without a word.

Frank's phone rang about 15 seconds later. He picked it up and responded in his most executive tone, "Yes?"

"Frank, is that you?" Sam asked.

Frank, becoming impatient, "Yes, of course it's me."

Frank heard a click and then began to talk to Bill, "So, how's the wife and kids?"

There was nothing but silence; then a dial tone.

Frank hung up in disbelief, as he thought, "$100,000, six months of careful planning and I'm sitting here *talking to myself*. 'How's the wife and kids'—sure, you want a phone system—cheap. Oh, yes, it's got features. It bakes bread and it even decides when to cut off customers so we don't appear too anxious to get their business."

---

It's not the most romantic subject, but everyone in today's business environment needs a solid telephone system for successful enterprise. Frank DeJames saw the urgent need to select an appropriate, up-to-date system to be sure his business had the competitive edge. So, he set up a meeting with Sam, his comptroller, and Sally, his office manager, to plan a comprehensive overhaul of the telephone system.

Frank started the meeting with the facts, "We are spending $40,000 a year on phones alone . . . it's just too much. I think we should be able to cut our costs and get some added benefits, too, if we buy rather than lease. I'm not sure how to get it done, but I want it done fast. We're just hemorrhaging too much cash!" All three decided they needed more information and made plans for Sam and Sally to attend a seminar on advanced phone systems. After the seminar, they set up another planning meeting where Frank announced he wanted a definite selection made within a month and the new system up and going in five months.

Sam was worried about the financial implications, "We really need a lot more financial data . . . more technical information too."

Sally had a lot of questions, no real answers and a growing sense of anxiety about making a hasty, unwise decision. "Most companies take a year to find a new phone system. We're going to do it in a month? The whole thing is too hurried; it's going to be chaotic. Besides, how can we learn enough about new technology . . . I'm worried we won't get all the important questions answered."

Frank always had a real sense for important issues that could produce visible advantages for the business. He could readily see that the phone system change would *ensure* more effective communication. He was a good delegater and thought he'd given Sally the resources, the time, and all the political backing she needed to get things done. However, Frank was not comfortable as a participant in day-to-day operations. Although Sam was a critical decision maker, he was basically a "facts and figures" man. He ran each of the options through his financial simulations to get the cost figures and then bowed out. With Frank bypassing the day-to-day activities and Sam only interested in the cost factors, Sally was left to fulfill all the other demands of the change process, both technical and managerial. She chose a vendor, arranged for training, and outlined a specific plan with a timeline to make sure things got done.

With Frank's protection, Sam's advice, and Sally's organization and persistence, most things worked—*almost!* The training was finished on time, but the outside vendor's experts didn't tailor the teaching to Frank's organization. There was too much information and not enough hands-on experience to master the system's basic functions. The implementation got done on time, but there was a lot of grumbling about all the extra trouble with the new system. Vital customers were put on hold indefinitely; the call forwarding procedure was confusing; and many complained that the personal touch—so much the hallmark of the consulting firm—disappeared with the message recording service.

Unfortunately, Frank only saw the big picture. He held another meeting with Sam and Sally to review how successful the change had proceeded. Frank emphasized the positive and rationalized the rough spots, "Changes take time. There's always some flack that you don't expect and can't predict. My rule of thumb is . . . it takes one year for any big change to pay off . . . by then the staff will know what to do and the change will begin to save time, money, and effort. You've got to push these things through or nothing gets done."

Sally said, "That's interesting. I wish you'd told me exactly what you expected from the beginning." Then she summed up the problems, "We needed better training. I didn't know enough of the technical details when we began and it would have helped to call in a technical expert. We also didn't get much buy-in from the staff. We didn't develop any believers in the system before we tried to implement it. We really didn't explain *why* we were making the change. Besides, the system has features people can't even pronounce, much less use. We don't even know if the staff needs these features."

Sam elaborated, "We needed to make it clear how the new system was going to help the business to be competitive. We did some things right, but if we had it to do over again, I should've covered some bases we didn't cover."

Sally, now getting revved up to speak her mind, added, "Yeah, it was crazy. I was either too busy to do a lot of what was needed or not the best person to do it."

Frank was unperturbed, as he responded, "You have to have a bias for action; you know, proactive interventions—not waiting until all the details are worked out. Just wait a little while and we'll get the bugs worked out."

Today all organizations must provide their employees with tools for personal productivity. As in many businesses, the leadership of this consulting firm envisioned that more office automation—a new phone system—would make each person more effective. Too often, however, management mandates the change and restricts its role to mustering the technical resources to implement it, overlooking what people need to understand to use the new system.

In particular, this change effort suffered from a significant lack of *several key roles*. The most effective change leaders do not suffer through hit-and-miss procedures by making changes with a team that is too limited. They methodically select a group of individuals that together have a range of skills. Frank started out with a circumstance with a significant chance of failure. He not only charged Sally with the job of managing the change, but also with mastering technical knowledge too. In addition, he did not assign anyone to assess whether or not this change was the best one to make, or anyone to sell the change to the organization, or anyone to respond to the needs of end users. In this chapter we will explore the roles that are critical for change and how to fill them.

## A QUESTION OF BALANCE

To assign roles in planned change efforts, a leader must match personal attributes with team role attributes *defined* in this chapter. As we outlined in Chapter 2, our research shows there are *six key team roles* that can meet most of the essential needs for *balanced* change.

1. *The Inventor,* who
   - Integrates trends and data into concepts, models and plans;
   - Envisions the big picture first; and
   - Adapts plans.

2. *The Entrepreneur,* who
   - Instinctively focuses on organizational efficiency and effectiveness;
   - Identifies critical issues and new possibilities; and
   - Actively seeks advantages and opportunities.
3. *The Integrator,* who
   - Forges alliances;
   - Gains personal acceptance, and acceptance for the team and their program; and
   - Relates practical plans to strategic plans and organizational issues.
4. *The Expert,* who
   - Takes responsibility for the technical knowledge and skills required for the change; and
   - Uses information skillfully and explains it in a logical way.
5. *The Manager,* who
   - Simplifies, delegates, assigns priorities; and
   - Develops others and gets the job done at all costs.
6. *The Sponsor,* who
   - Ensures support and resources from the highest levels of the organization; and
   - Communicates where the change fits in the organizational vision.

We will refer to the roles as a *team,* because they are dependent on one another and work together cohesively in the change process. However, it is not necessary for the players to meet together as a working group. If the communication between them is effective, the players can work independently with the change leader *coordinating* their common effort.

Sharing leadership is often difficult for many senior managers. After all, the traditional image is of a leader who is firmly in control. To give up control to a "group" may be democratic, but not typical of American leaders. However, the most successful change teams we observed had the six roles covered with the leadership distributed among team members. This does not require six individuals. Instead, in some cases, roles may be shared; in other cases one person may perform more than one role. However, those assigned the roles are held accountable for their contributions. The most successful change leaders employ systematic feedback procedures to see how the team is functioning. While contributions from each individual role are vital, the attributes of all six roles are combined to fulfill team goals.

How can a leader motivate people with the right talents and combine their individual skills to implement change? The critical factor is to enlist those with specific competencies to introduce the change. Sometimes a demanding change effort challenges individuals in a way that clarifies their capacity to fulfill specific roles. However, there is no simple formula for choosing change-team roles. Leaders must *discover and understand* the concrete qualities inherent in each person and *sense* how to use these human resources to assemble the skills for change. They have the responsibility to utilize those who are already available and to secure additional talent. A well-respected major league baseball manager was asked about his "strategy" when he replaced a key hitter with another player to bunt in the bottom of the ninth during a very close game. He replied: "In baseball there is no such thing as strategy. It's all a matter of getting the right players into the right situation every day. If they do the job, you're a hero. If they don't, you're a bum." This attitude about talent is also critical for effective change.

The competencies required for effective change are most often distributed among several people in an organization. One general manager who was in charge of several manufacturing plants remarked:

> I sometimes get frustrated when I can't get the skills I need where I need them. My guy in Florida is very innovative. I really like his problem-solving style. But, I also really respect my manager in Michigan. He's not as flamboyant, but he quietly gets the job done and he keeps very careful track of the numbers. A lot of days I wish I had both of them combined into one person.

Some leaders select team members by criteria such as job title or technical proficiencies. Some assign members on the basis of their availability. Many are assigned their change teams without choice. In all cases, a competent leader assures adequate role coverage. This may require enlisting individuals from outside the formal team; assigning the responsibility for a set of role attributes to someone who has the potential, but not the natural competence; or sharing responsibillity among team members for uncovered roles. Often, one person plays more than one role. For example, someone may aggressively push through a change idea and deal with political concerns at the same time. No matter what the nature of the formal team, change leaders ensure that all necessary roles are covered by competent individuals who can work together.

## GENERATOR OF IDEAS: THE INVENTOR

*Inventors* initiate new thoughts and processes. They *originate, create, discover.* Inventors foster an exploratory climate—searching for different methods and unexplored possibilities. They *experiment* and *test;* they *persist* until solutions to problems are found and perspectives widened. For example, in the case of the engineering consulting firm, no one saw the need for an inventor. Do you really require one when the change effort is so well defined? In most instances—yes! The inventor would have asked whether or not they were making the *right* change. He or she would have instinctively searched for a better technology to make consultants more productive individually, both *before* and *after* installing the phone system.

An innovative CEO told us his secret for success in generating new possibilities in manufacturing—*a specific person* who spent full time projecting future events and plans:

> Some people wonder what Jack does. He hasn't been really successful at managing anything ever. Some people think he must have a special "in" with me. He spends a large part of his efforts *gathering information*—information about future economic possibilities, trends in the changing marketplace, and new approaches in product development found elsewhere. He has an uncanny ability to get out there and find out what's happening, and from that, he lets his imagination wander until he anticipates events. One of my VPs once suggested I could reduce "head

count" by replacing Charlie with a crystal ball, but the other thing I like about him is his ability to match what he's thinking about to concrete *current* plans. He doesn't forget the steps between his new insights and today's daily effort. He can imagine the unimaginable, but at the same time, he remembers that we live in the "here and now."

*An inventor is an innovator who solves problems in a new and unforeseen way.* This is the interpretation of the engineer who oversees the technical operation of an international air freight operation. He believes that many inventive ideas grow out of *necessity* and *survival,* as he describes how necessity drove him to solve a major problem:

Transporting freight all over the world, we often have trouble with fog delaying our shipments when pilots can't land on time at their destinations. Since the invention of the airplane, pilots have been looking for a way to fly through fog. The solutions always have been to design systems that eliminate the need for the pilot to see and have machines that "see." As a result, we have always had complex systems to land planes by using on-the-ground electronic equipment. Many times these systems don't work. We were frustrated about the complaints customers had when shipments were delayed. We looked everywhere for solutions, including going to Paris to inspect the big machines that blow fog off the runways. These damn machines cost $12 million each! Then I learned that the Air Force uses millimeter-wave radar to take pictures through clouds and a United States company is investing tons of money to install the components in their planes . . . to *see* through fog. We can't invest tons of capital in the fancy components, but we can put the pilot back in charge of *looking,* rather than machines *"looking."* I started our pilots using an old-fashioned, but improved, radar device to do their own "peering" through the fog. It's not perfect, but our freight is beginning to arrive on time ninety-five percent of the time.

*Inventors keep posing "what if" to a number of people.* They are the individuals who imagine the long-term implications of new technologies and processes. The origin of the transistor that revolutionized many modern-day communications was imagined and dreamed about a generation before it became a reality. The what-ifs of the transistor made it possible to come forth *suddenly* with dozens of uses for it, which would not have been possible had the dreams and simulations not preceded its introduction. Developing what-if approaches requires that inventors draw on all aspects of their imagination.

## SEEING THE LIGHT

One technician described how he created a new idea for embedding filaments in glass for light bulbs "The representatives of the manufacturer were giving me a demonstration on a new manufacturing process for making light bulbs. They rolled the glass over the filaments; it didn't work too well. I began to have trouble following their presentation. I kept wondering if there was a better way. I began asking some questions and throwing out a bunch of ideas. We didn't even finish the demonstration. But we did come up with the simplest and best idea. We wanted a filament imbedded in glass that looked like it was 'pinched' between two fingers—not rolled flat—so we designed a 'pinching machine' right on the spot."

*Inventors use other people regularly and consistently to redefine how products and services fit into the marketplace.* This is more than brainstorming. It is an *analysis of the status quo* with the specific intention of inventing new approaches.

## MANAGEMENT BY PETTY DETAILS

A manager of engineering at a consumer products company told us how he came up with a new product design: "I went around to marketing and asked them to be real petty—come up with every detail that bothered them about the x-1 product line. I did the same with manufacturing. I went to the group management meetings and got them to rank what approaches were most important to them—cost reduction, market share, technological leadership, etcetera. Then I sat down with my guys and some people from marketing and manufacturing and we tried to figure out what we should do over the next year. As we were sitting there, it came to me . . . if we could move the heat element about 45 degrees and reduce its size without decreasing performance, then we could have a double-use product—combine x-1 and x-2. That would reduce costs in manufacturing and get over a problem that marketing said really bugged the customer."

*Inventors put themselves in the center of organizational problem-solving activity,* communicating frequently with internal and external experts to define and solve problems. They take an extensive inventory of existing problems and conceptual gaps and *analyze* them to uncover new ways of removing inherent stumbling blocks. Often this process can take months or years of gathering information, probing into new possibilities, and experimenting with others in the organization. A research scientist at a computer firm reported the following experience:

I came up with an idea for a new kind of memory chip. I spent a few months working alone, but then saw the necessity to put a team together. I had to test my concepts with other people, because I was just too close to my ideas to get a sense of whether or not they'd work!

The idea of a scientist or engineer inventing and accomplishing innovations *singly* is a dangerous stereotype. Most often it is the technical and people skills acquired throughout a career that enables inventors to inspire and lead teams into an inventive, creative climate to come up with a new breakthrough. The team effort is usually far more productive than a solo performance.

*Successful inventors develop the habit of searching widely* in and out of their own sphere of operation for new ideas. They never remove themselves from the mainstream—sitting alone somewhere (in a lab or attic) dreaming up new concepts. They need the stimulation of comparing their own creative thinking with the creativity and originality of others. Planned innovations often fail from the "not-invented-here syndrome." Outstanding inventors seldom participate in this kind of thinking. Instead, they frequently secure suggestions from outside their immediate circle of influence (e.g., colleagues, members of other organizational departments, competitors, and the popular scientific and trade literature). Alexander Graham Bell, a Scotsman who came to Boston to teach the deaf, not to become an inventor, repeatedly said that he could never have invented the telephone without the exchange of ideas with a number of inventors in other parts of the world who were actually as close as he to making a functioning telephone.

*Effective inventors are not afraid to learn from failure.* They try over and over again; they persist in their efforts, disciplining themselves not to become discouraged.

### GOOD IDEAS NEVER DIE

A systems analyst in an insurance company implemented a sales reporting system with sales executives, using portable computers in the field. He told us how he came up with the concept in the first place: "In the late sixties I had tried to develop a more formal tracking and reporting system. Of course, that was in the days before microprocessors. More forms had to be sent back to headquarters. The sales managers balked and their antipathy was enough to discourage the current VP for sales. Then in the seventies a new VP for sales wanted better coordination of key account strategies, so I designed this system that ran on the minicomputer of each office or region linked to headquarters. I remember I was complimented by a data processing magazine for having a progressive system. But that one, too, wasn't that successful. The VP for sales never overcame some of the political problems with key account management between regions. Then last year some of the same concerns came up, so they approached me again. This time I had the idea of using portable computers, but I built the screen exactly like the forms that the salespeople carried around anyway and gave them some tools to do analyses *on the spot* with prospects. They love that. As far as the reporting and telecommunication go, I had solved these problems years ago with those other systems, so I just updated what we had developed over the last 20 years. I'm a strong believer that no good ideas are ever wasted. It's just a matter of time to get them connected to something really useful. That is why an initial failure shouldn't throw you!"

*Inventors look for new ways of re-using concepts that are already in operation to discover new possibilities.* They suspend judgment until they have tried new concepts with a cross section of people and adapted them to new settings. Open-mindedness makes it possible to see new aspects of old situations and conditions. Many inventions are merely *variations* of old and proven products and processes that grew from an inventor's "looking with a different vision."

*Inventors have a sense of timing* for introducing new products and processes. A vice-president of human resources for a medium-sized company told us how he planned the right time for introducing a new incentive system for senior executives:

One night I sat down and worked one up at home. I kept refining it until I thought that the numbers made sense. But I didn't introduce it at that time. I knew there was too much attachment to the old one. Then after a meeting where we discussed next year's business plans, someone asked how we were going to get people to carry out a new direction. I knew it was the *right time* to suggest we look at the incentive system.

*Inventors are "projectionists"—always looking to the future to solve problems that have not yet surfaced.* This kind of looking ahead is usually done with others to ensure relevancy rather than as a lone performer removed from reality.

**To summarize:**

---

If your change effort needs an *inventor*, look for people who
- Informally test the waters for new ideas with a variety of people;
- Continually redefine existing business issues and problems;
- Come up with new ideas that they do not cling to as their own, but allow others to take them on, expand them, and create further imaginative concepts;
- Relate any plans and strategies they initiate to aggressive initiatives that are relevant and timely; and
- Anticipate future events and develop concepts and plans to meet them.

---

## FINDING A BETTER WAY: THE ENTREPRENEUR

The *entrepreneur organizes* and *manages resources* to maximize for opportunites for innovation. Entrepreneurs can come from any level in an organization. In fact, the most successful organizations have entrepreneurs at all levels.

*Entrepreneurs drive the change process.* In the consulting firm case about selecting a new phone system, the lack of an individual to "sell" the change was a critical deficit. Without someone to show how features of the phone system could improve business performance, the project was unlikely to achieve wide success. In more technically oriented change programs, leaders often mobilize inventors who do not have skills to propel their own creations through the organization. These idea people, gifted in coming up with technological innovations, need entrepreneurs to frame them into a change initiative.

*Entrepreneurs constantly search for better products and work practices.* They are the primary proponents of change as a normal and healthy habit. A new plant manager told us:

When I took over my new assignment, I noticed that there were more than one hundred forms just to track inventory around the plant. I said there just had to be a better way. Then I went to a conference in Chicago and saw a demonstration of a computer-driven manufacturing information system. I knew right away we had to have that here in our operation.

The hallmark of the entrepreneur is the constant search for new and better ways of running operations. Unlike the inventor, who is more concerned with *creating* something new, entrepreneurs will adapt ideas gleaned *from any source* to make improvements and ensure success.

*Successful entrepreneurs frame their concepts to "sell."* They are constantly engaged in *promoting* new ideas and approaches. In working with others, they are master presenters and master influencers who excite, motivate, and mobilize others to reach common goals. They seek opportunities to introduce their innovations at the right time and in the right setting to gain acceptance.

### FIND THE RIGHT PLACE

A chemical plant engineer we interviewed, told us about introducing a new instrumentation system. "I guess I was sort of a maniac for a few months. I constantly looked for any opportunity and *the right place* to introduce the new system. I remember one day one of the foremen complained that his life would be lot better if he could trust the reading from his gauges and not have to send a man out to inspect the pump, as the safety rules specified. We ended the conversation with both of us speculating how wonderful the world would be if only someone would invent a digital readout from a computer monitoring the exact condition in that area of the plant. I think when I came back with the approval from management to start installing the new instrumentation system, the foreman thought I was some kind of genius and he continued to boast about how he had given me the idea."

*Entrepreneurs develop networks of people for testing ideas and generating new possibilities.* Entrepreneurs have the ability to recognize and utilize resources wherever they can be found and mobilize a variety of talented people to join in the change effort. Those we interviewed were especially effective at utilizing the talents and special skills of others to accomplish their goals. Sometimes they do this in an informal, spontaneous setting.

### FIND THE RIGHT PEOPLE
One entrepreneur told us about a time when he was searching for the application of a particular invention that his research laboratory had made: "I was pretty sure that the market analysis my people had done was wrong. One evening we were having cocktails with a new neighbor, who is a surgeon. It suddenly struck me that there was a medical application. A day or so later, I asked the surgeon if I could visit him in the hospital. I prepared some specific questions to ask him, mainly centering around postsurgery problems. He complained about a procedure for removing sutures. I began asking him some 'what if' questions. Then I hit on it. I knew we had an application for the new polymer. I redirected the whole effort and I still use the surgeon to test ideas that come up in the development phase."

*Entrepreneurs look for reasonably challenging goals, not high-risk change projects.* Entrepreneurs are often portrayed as high-risk takers. However, our research shows that outstanding entreprenuers avoid changes with a significant chance of failure. Many entreprenuers gauge the difficulty of projects by instinctively breaking them down into discrete steps. This procedure helps them judge to what extent resources are available to complete change. External observers see them as taking risky steps, because the discrete steps that assure moderate risk are often not manifest.

*Entrepreneurs use vision and goal-setting to keep others mobilized.* They are adept at helping others visualize the concrete outcomes from change. By breaking the vision down into concrete goals, objectives, and steps, the entrepreneur helps others understand the direction of the planned change, their potential role in it, and the payoff for the organization. The best entrepreneurs translate their visions into practical initiatives to mobilize others.

*Entrepreneurs see obstacles as opportunities.*

### HOW I CHANGED MY OFFICE JOB
### INTO A FIELD DAY

A senior military officer described his experience of being sent to an "office job" in the middle of his career: "When I came down to Washington, I thought that this must be the most 'unfun' place in the whole world. In the field I was always inventing new challenges. Here I thought I would just push paper all day. Then one day when we were doing a review of a project I had previously thought rather boring, I had the idea that this program could actually be very helpful, if we could extend it into the field. I spent the next two years pushing through that program. I think that I've got to say that it is one of the most successful, highly supported nonweapons system in the entire military."

*Entrepreneurs take an inventory of all available resources—people, processes, products—to determine the potential for success.* They transform opportunities into realistic plans that produce results. Entrepreneurs obtain necessary resources from outside and inside the organization to accomplish their objectives.

**To summarize:**

---

If your change effort needs an *entrepreneur,* look for someone who is good at
- Experimenting with and introducing innovations that result in improved efficiency and effectiveness;
- Seeing opportunities to influence others and obtain their early support for projects;

- Getting others involved in projects early and delegating key segments of the projects;
- Seeing opportunities in situations where significant obstacles are present; and
- Gathering resources—people, ideas, financial and political support—to accomplish goals.

---

## PUTTING IT ALL TOGETHER: THE INTEGRATOR

An *integrator* is the person who takes parts and fragments of the change process and weaves them into a coordinated whole. Organizations are composed of people pulled in multiple directions. The integrator finds the common thread among diverse interests. A senior manager pointed out to us, "One of the confusing things about running an organization is that people are always clamoring for change, yet whenever any change is proposed, it breeds new forms of resistance." Integrators skillfully bypass this resistance—recognizing both the personal issues and organizational themes that create it. They move instinctively across political boundaries to make people feel at ease. Integrators ensure the coordination of critical elements in the change process. A wise manager described his role as "similar to the functions that take place in electrical cells—the coordination of the *receptor, connector,* and *effector.*" The integrator *receives* the information and existing facts, *connects* them to the whole, and proceeds to be the *effector* by *creating a total, coordinated effort.* In the case describing the consulting firm's selection of a telephone system, there was no integrator. This role vulnerability impaired implementation of the phone system substantially. That company needed someone who could answer concerns of potential end users, who could get buy-in by showing how the system would fit into overall business strategies, and who could mobilize various constituencies for collaboration and support.

*Integrators reframe ideas or put information into a new context to stimulate new perspectives.* Unlike the entrepreneur who creates "added value" for the organization, the integrator's instinct is to gain acceptance of change. One integrator described his role in the following way:

It's my job to be sure we take the data and information that are available and not have it misused through misinterpretation or careless application. Often, history indicates directions for the present and the future. My real task is to help the team review the past, size up the present, formulate new plans that take care of the here and now and provide for the future.

*Integrators bring together diverse groups of people to achieve success.* They accomplish this through the skillful use of an array of interpersonal strategies, such as *sharing, information-gathering, listening, getting feedback,* and *clarifying concepts.* In addition, they instinctively take the time to establish rapport and show respect for others, focusing on the needs and concerns of others. Integrators *blend* the talents and abilities of the team members into a productive working unit by mobilizing groups to use information to overcome prejudices, preconceived notions, or other stumbling blocks to innovation. In this way, they create "running room" for the inventor and entrepreneur to launch their ideas.

Failure to have an integrator involved in a change effort often results in political conflicts so intense that they divert energy away from the change process. This can be disastrous. At best, it may take much longer to bring about change, because potentially helpful key constituencies are not mobilized or because factions opposed to the change are not persuaded to cooperate.

*Skillful integrators form solid alliances* by not separating themselves from critical issues or key people. Their talent for keeping the overall picture of change in mind helps them to cement alliances effectively and build cohesive teams. By maintaining their network of relationships, integrators serve as a bridge for diverse interests. In addition, they anticipate resistance and prepare contingency plans for overcoming concerns.

## OVERCOMING RESISTANCE

One integrator described how he overcame resistance: "I knew that the middle-level line managers were deeply suspicious of any effort to form quality circles. They felt it usurped their traditional 'right' to manage. At a meeting, I explained that my role wasn't to serve the hourly workers or the union. I represented the company and I wanted to make sure that any of the quality or other improvement programs we had going met their needs as managers. So I got them to list what they saw as the things that most needed improvement, both in the work setting, as well as the product. Although they expressed some things differently, a lot of issues were very similar to the quality circles issues. Whenever we worked on an issue that needed their help, I would refer to the list. I tried to break down the 'us versus them' environment. That really helped."

*Integrators build teams and develop group identity around the change effort.* They continually practice informal networking, coalition, and alliance-building by cultivating allies to support their special interests. One marketing manager told us:

I was having a lot of trouble getting the manufacturing people to adopt a change in our product, particularly the manager of production. By chance, one day I was traveling in the airport limo with one of his coworkers. By some of the things the coworker was saying, I could see that he wasn't too happy about some aspects of the product either. Rather than sell him on our proposal right there, I suggested he talk with Tom, one of my product support managers, about what distributors were saying. Perhaps this information could help us. I checked with Tom a week or so later and he told me that he had met with manufacturing several times. Amazingly, at the next staff meeting, the production manager was actually making our proposal for us. I just sat back and supported him.

*Integrators have the role of maintaining the "protected" status of the change project within the organization.* They develop a sense for the formal and informal boundaries in the organization, the critical players and their major interests. They focus on the *issues* that are most important to different people, the *dangers* in pushing certain strategies, and the *outcomes* that are possible with different groups. Integrators are a primary force in mediation, negotiation, and healthy compromise.

*Integrators confront conflict and clarify distortions.* They develop the public speaking skills for larger group functions, effective one-to-one communication for relationship-building, and writing skills for the quick and wide distribution of information. These attributes help integrators *clarify, interpret, inform, update,* and *summarize key issues from disparate sources.* In addition, integrators define the crux of an issue, eliminating extraneous details. This helps them distill information into its most useful form. These skills are critical to building the kind of credibility necessary to bring all factions together. A manufacturing engineer described how she built credibility in implementing a factory automation project:

> Once we actually started the installation of the equipment, I knew the workers would have questions that had not occurred before. I made it a point to be down on the shop floor first thing every morning to answer these. If I didn't have an answer, I posted the question on a board and made sure I found someone who could answer it *that day.*"

*Integrators cultivate counseling and information-gathering skills to clarify the concerns of change-team members.* They take the time to "hear" the concerns of those on the team and offer necessary support. They have an openness that invites dialogue and a presence that makes coworkers feel respected and validated.

## LISTEN AND "HEAR"

A divisional general manager related this anecdote: "After we reorganized, I got a lot of bad vibes from the very group whose brand would gain the most from the reorganization. It didn't seem rational, so I talked to the brand manager and some of his staff. Mostly, I just listened and tried to put myself in their shoes. As it turned out, their worst fear was the possibility of losing control. They didn't believe they really had the authority to push their brand in the new setting; and I could see their point. I talked my colleagues into making sure that all the brand managers were represented at divisional meetings."

*The integrator is the chief informer, major communicator, and presenter to top management, allies, the change team, and end users.* Bringing together each of these components becomes a daily challenge. In addition, the integrators assess and inform key personnel about available and needed resources. They coordinate diverse efforts by presenting an overall "picture" of what people are thinking and doing.

**To summarize:**

---

If your change effort needs an *integrator,* look for someone who is good at
- Using an understanding of others' positions to form alliances,
- Identifying key issues and themes from diverse sources and interpreting their importance,
- Correctly judging how far the "politics" of organizational issues need to be pursued,
- Bringing together diverse elements in the organization, and
- Coordinating all activities with a solid effort that produces results.

---

## MAKING IT TECHNICALLY CORRECT: THE EXPERT

An *expert* is the person who is a specialist, proficient and skilled in specific technical areas of the change effort. Sally, principally working alone with her new telephone system implementation, had to "bootleg" expertise by educating herself at seminars. A vulnerable tactic, at best, it unfortunately made her comfortable enough to proceed, but not knowledgeable enough to avoid major technical pitfalls. In fact, by depending on outside vendors she didn't know, the company got inadequate advice and inappropriate encouragement.

*An expert is the person on the change team who has mastered skills through special training or experience and contributes special proficiency and competence.* A high-tech company employed its own programmers to introduce the computerization of conveyor belts. However, it soon became apparent that additional expertise was needed to change the entire system quickly enough for it to be cost effective. An outside, skilled technician came in and quickly introduced untried, innovative methods. The in-house programmers learned from the outside technician and rapidly became "inside" experts.

In this age of specialization, experts' skills are prerequisite for technical changes. They ensure that past mistakes are corrected, present plans defined, and future projections made. Specialists point out the specific paths for making the change journey.

*Experts are the connection between the specialized information required for change implementation and those who eventually have to live with the change.* Therefore, they must be able to work with others and interpret their technical skill in practical terms to the change team and the entire organization.

Controversy exists about whether to use internal or external experts or both in change efforts. Since lack of technical knowledge may kill a project, the first priority is to ensure that *the appropriate knowledge is available,* no matter what the source. That often means going outside of the organization. However, outside experts who do not have ongoing relationships with key personnel in the organization may hinder, not help, the change. Often in-house experts who understand the organization's needs, but who may not know the latest technology, can become "technical partners"—the outside expert provides the knowledge; the inside experts translate and design applications.

Speed is often a vital consideration. But, if the change effort extends over time, building a cadre of experts within the organization may be appropriate. If the change is a one-time application of technical wisdom or of short duration, using outside experts may be more expedient, particularly if their contributions are unusual or unique. Criteria for *collaborating with outside experts* include

1.  Specifying the change before approaching outside experts;
2.  Conducting a broad search before narrowing your choices;
3.  Evaluating potential experts' experience with change efforts similar to yours;
4.  Ensuring that the expert *understands* your technical needs and your organization;
5.  Thoroughly reviewing suggestions, goals, plans, timelines, project staffing, and potential problems;
6.  Developing contingency plans for potential problems with the expert;
7.  Developing informal and formal types of leverage for ensuring the quality and time-lines of the expert's work;
8.  Regularly reviewing the expert's input; and
9.  Piloting products/processes provided by experts with likely end users.

By developing rules for managing outside experts, change leaders can avoid losing control of their projects and can guarantee enough support for outside personnel.

*Experts have one or more unique skills resulting from special training or experience.* Companies are beginning to see the need for training their own employees in specialized fields and for offering them adequate pay and status for pursuing specialties. A growing number of high-tech companies are taking a fresh look at dual career ladders—promotion systems that reward highly creative laboratory and research personnel with the same salaries, titles, and perks as those usually reserved for managers. As corporations recommit themselves to long-term product and process innovations, they have begun to provide career paths that keep experts in their laboratories, rather than seeking managerial posts for higher pay and recognition. A senior researcher at a computer firm who has registered 135 American patents for his company in 34 years, stated that he has been very happy as an expert called in to assist management: "Twenty years ago, I was offered a management job; I have thanked myself a thousand times for saying no. I've served my company so much better as a researcher—as a resource person managers can call on."

Dual career paths apply to nonresearch experts too. For example, an information technology firm installed a dual career ladder for its sales force. Outstanding salespeople stay in the field as they move up through four different job levels, each with higher salaries and perks. The higher-level personnel aren't managers, but they are expected to do more than sell—to train people, help in market research, field-test new products, or expand larger territories. One executive labeled them as "on-the-job experts"—a vital component—called in regularly to share their know-how.

*Experts periodically update implementors of change and end users* about progress, objective efforts, and specific results.

### THREE OUT OF FIVE AIN'T BAD

A systems analyst told us this story: "I always make sure that before I present a computer screen to an end user, I check it. If I see five problems with it and I can easily fix three, I'll just leave two not fixed. After all, when we have the meeting and I've fixed them, then the user will say those two things are wrong . . . can't you fix those? I'll have to say, 'Perhaps, but it will take a while'. On the other hand, if I fix nothing, then when they see the five problems, I can tell them these three are easy to fix, but the other two are more of a problem. In the first case, the user goes away with 100 percent of their claims not met; in the latter, they have 60 percent met!"

*Experts maintain an open dialogue with end users,* not only to ensure the relevance of their work, but also to set the tone for adopting new ideas and innovative methods.

### MAKING IT FIT THE JOB

A factory automation expert related this example: "While we were working on the shop floor taking measurements of everything, I got into a conversation with the foreman and a couple of the workers. After a week or so when we became quite friendly, I asked them about some of the things that were going on in the unit. As the foreman described his viewpoint, it became apparent to me that doing the implementation the way we were doing it was not going to solve any of this guy's problems, even though he had never objected to the plans. Perhaps he didn't understand them. I told my boss that we should alter our plan and put in the parts' tracking system first. It wasn't a big deal technically, but it meant a lot to that foreman, and I knew that we would get a lot of help from him afterwards."

*Experts cultivate effective presentation and communication skills to transfer their knowledge and unique contribution to the team effort.* A large insurance company in the Midwest employed an expert in the field of family health to study in-house data and come up with a means of interpreting the data both to staff and clients. The expert was unusually skilled at assembling the data, but he lacked the necessary skills in presentation to make his material meaningful. A specialist can be self-defeating and can undermine change by what one perceptive executive described as "interpreting his know-how only to himself. He might as well talk to himself rather than *confuse* and *demoralize* the whole group."

*Competent experts present complex ideas in terms related to the end users' concerns.* They not only make sure the language is tailored to the audience, but also take into account *how* the audience learns or absorbs concepts. We observed, in presentations about complex change, that average performers use flowcharts, technical terms, or detailed documentation with end users. They frequently "firehose" audiences with overwhelming data. In contrast, superior experts tend to disperse information in very concrete terms, specifically focused on the discrete impact the change will produce.

*Experts employ specific methods for problem detection.* The speed with which trained specialists can detect and solve problems is the greatest asset they have. Often this speed applied at the right moment can prevent countless critical mistakes.

*Experts ensure the most up-to-date and contemporary procedures in specialized areas.* Outstanding experts find ways to keep abreast of new discoveries or methods in their field. They are not afraid to ask for help, either within or outside of the organization, nor to utilize that which is most current and timely.

*Experts are the key persons who care for the technical details of the project and provide the interface between change implementors and the entire organization.* They are the resource for dramatic changes in technology and apply current insight to save the organization time and money.

**To summarize:**

---

If your change effort needs an *expert,* look for people who are good at
- Using their specialized technical knowledge in the *key* areas of the change implementation;
- Collecting up-to-date information that others use to solve problems and make decisions;
- Using well-researched data-based methods; and
- Systematically bringing to the change effort new approaches, grounded in a special expertise.

---

## KEEPING THINGS ON TRACK: THE MANAGER

A *manager* is the administrator, the guide, the regulator, and the stimulator who motivates the team to work for a common goal. As an administrator, the manager directs and controls the activities of key personnel without being authoritarian. Managers give guidance by simplifying and delegating tasks; they set priorities and outline goals to be accomplished; and they effectively coach others to complete key tasks. In the case about the consulting firm selecting a new telephone system, Sally filled the role of manager well. She assigned priorities, developed her knowledge and that of others, and made sure the job got done.

A manager in a large computer manufacturer held several management positions in marketing and financial planning and then was promoted to the position of controller of the national accounts division. She was asked what she considered a good manager. She said:

> The textbooks call it *optimizing the human resource,* but I think it is bringing out the best in people. We have three basic beliefs that form our value system. First, we strive for excellence in everything we do. Second, we try to provide the best possible service to our customers. And third, we respect the individual . . . all the time, and not just when it is expedient. There are hundreds of people in my organization, so it's clear that I can't do their jobs for them, so I have to rely on their ability to do the job well . . . I let them know that if they do a good job, they will be recognized individually and as members of a winning team. Whether it is a pat on the back, a cash award or a promotion, we all need to know that our work has value and is appreciated . . . and that we can succeed, based on the merits of our work.

One of the major responsibilities of a manager is to create this kind of climate. Failure to have a manager of the change team often results in missing project deadlines or a poor implementation of plans. It may seem obvious that someone has to manage tasks, but many projects fail because no one plays this specific role or because this responsibility is dispersed too widely in the organization.

*Managers are the rudders of the entire change team; they bring together the best practices of the group on a daily basis.* They oversee the day-by-day implementation by monitoring results and setting new objectives. In technically oriented change projects, managers and others frequently become overinvolved in details. The best managers resist this temptation, delegating key tasks to all team members and specialists. Through hands-on participation and coaching, managers develop the skills of coworkers. Most importantly, managers enhance team spirit by generating the feeling that "we're all in the effort together." In particular, the managers *reward* the contributions of team members openly and frequently with concrete and visible evidence of a job well done.

*Managers are the agents for increasing employee productivity and raising the quality of employee output.* In any change effort, managers must maintain a balance between two activities—(1) attending to the needs of employees; and (2) assuring that work progresses. Less successful managers tend to overemphasize one or the other, either becoming oversolicitous of employees' concerns or totally preoccupied with completing tasks. The most successful managers consistently balance goal completion and worker satisfaction. This means creating an effective work plan before work begins and modifying the plan as the work progresses to meet changing demands.

*Managers carefully weigh the resources and time required to innovate against the risk of not completing the implementation successfully.* While the entrepreneur may make calculated risks for a total venture, once it is under way, effective managers assume responsibility for project completion. Implementing on time is one of their major objectives. They are sensitive to the need to provide for unseen "glitches" in the implementation and anticipate the need for modifications and adjustments in the change plan.

## CHOOSE THE RIGHT TIME

A project manager for a large automated hospital claims system related this experience with one of his computer software engineers: "Anne came back from a course out West really fired up. She said that she really wanted to try a new method of writing a computer code. I told her it was a good idea—it was a better way, but we had a *deadline* in two weeks and we had to make that! I asked her what we would lose by not using the new method immediately. She listed some losses, but I didn't think they were great enough to go to the customer and announce we had to delay the agreed-upon deadline. I told her that I was enthusiastic about her trying out the new method, but I asked her to make plans for doing it later. Although I had sent her on the course for her benefit and for the benefit of the organization, we'd have to integrate the new practice after we kept our promise to the customer. So, we agreed she'd run a course about the new method for other team members before the beginning of the next project phase."

*Effective managers of change efforts focus on end results.* To do this, they document and update change plans and publicize plan revisions on a regular basis. In addition, they develop ways to track projects, intervening quickly to take care of the small emotional and functional problems that sometimes throw project teams off track.

*Successful managers find ways to involve others.* They emphasize acquiring the right blend of team skills. Managers recognize that doing the work themselves can be especially demotivating to employees. The biggest temptation for managers (especially those who are technically skilled) is to get involved in doing the work themselves, when a project is off track. The "watch me, then follow" style of management may work well with tremendously energetic, self-motivated managers, but it usually undermines team motivation.

*Good managers give appropriate "backing" to their subordinates,* even though they may not involve themselves in the details of a project. Sometimes they give specific coaching on how to improve a task. At other times, managers simply need to listen to problems and issues and offer tangible support. Often their support is manifest in simply building the confidence of team members.

## TANGIBLE SUPPORT

The assistant vice-president of a products group in a major bank reported, "I knew that John was blocked in a particular aspect of the project. He needed help from the treasury group. Even though he had a good relationship with that group, nothing seemed to happen. Eventually he came around to tell me that the manager in treasury was not offering support. He wanted me to talk to the manager. I told him I thought it was a bad idea; he'd never have any credibility if I intervened whenever obstacles came up. I told him I understood the problem of dealing with someone at different levels in the organization and suggested that he call a meeting with some of their people to discuss progress on the project and that he invite me and the treasury manager to sit in. During the meeting, I said nothing. As the meeting concluded, the manager of treasury revealed that he understood the project, for the first time, and asked what we needed from his organization. John smiled at me and then told him. The manager said, 'Fine. You've got it!' "

**To summarize:**

---

If your change effort needs a *manager,* look for someone who is good at
- Defining, communicating, and tracking plans;
- Introducing well-tested changes to work procedures as situations require them;
- Focusing on getting the job done efficiently without letting personal feelings interfere with the drive toward the end result;
- Identifying team members to whom responsibilities can be delegated;
- Coaching others about how to improve their performance; and
- Consolidating talents and skills to achieve clearly defined goals.

---

## SUPPORT FROM ABOVE: THE SPONSOR

As we discussed in Chapter 4, obtaining support from top management is critical to ensuring general organizational readiness for a change. The sponsor is vital for sustaining this support.

*The sponsor is the person in higher management who ensures that the change effort has broad organizational support and resources.* Sponsors use their status and political "clout" in the organization to eliminate serious obstacles. Frank DeJames, the CEO in the consulting firm that selected the new phone system, sponsored the change. On the surface, he was a vigorous supporter. However, as many upper-level leaders, he gave a mandate and essentially bowed out. Instead, he should have provided resources, his ongoing energy, and visibility. Sponsors use their status and political clout in the organization to eliminate serious obstacles.

### USING "CLOUT"

A senior manager of a large multinational company, described how his change project got a sponsor: "We worked for months coming up with formal plans for a new venture. I was prepared and my people were prepared. The proposal had to get the executive committee's approval before going on to the board. The only obstacle was that the vice-president in charge of the electronics sector saw the change as part of his business area. I hadn't been able to convince him that it was a completely new business that couldn't use any production or distribution channels his sector controlled. I knew he was not going to publicly oppose it. He'd just stonewall, probably around the budget issue. That is exactly what happened. For a while it looked like others weren't going to go for the new venture. That's when the CEO gave his input. He told the executive committee that he thought this was the most important project for the company in years and proposed a way of dealing with the budget that got around all the electronics sector's arguments. I nearly jumped up and hugged him on the spot. Thereafter, the CEO continued his active support—not by substantive direct involvement, but by providing ongoing, visible input in resources, feedback, and public acknowledgment."

The idea of "obtaining top management support" has become a modern cliché. Nevertheless, in our experience, some middle managers develop a pressing desire to push through change on their own. When the process seems so obviously beneficial, they often ignore the need for higher-level support and fail. One middle-level manager with whom we were consulting remarked, "If I had to wait for top-level support for every change I make, I would never make any changes." Although this was essentially true, several selective problems in major programs under this manager's direction never got solved, because they did not have *the resources or credibility top management could provide.*

Most often change efforts that do not have sponsors fail when they run into top-level political problems. Even when they are successful, sponsorless projects take longer, because they lack a means of confronting higher-level obstacles.

*Sponsors are the top-management enthusiasts who fight for the project and who are willing to lend their credibility to ensure its completion.* They may not be the top functional managers in a change project, but they are the "godparents" of it. Senior managers often resist taking on this role, since it requires committing corporate resources. They may also hesitate to offer support because of political factors, or they may feel they may have to take on added responsibilities and problems. Change leaders should choose sponsors who are energetic, responsible about following through with commitments, and have the courage to lend their influence.

*Successful sponsors are skilled at justifying to top management the rationale behind the change and relating it to change plans.* They not only specify reasons for innovation, but also show exactly how individual events or steps in the process fit with overall goals of the project. One sponsor described a particularly acrimonious telephone conversation with the general manager of another division:

> He thought that his division was the only one that was going to have the new technology. It's true his division had given us some start-up funds. But, I reminded him of a meeting where we agreed that we had to distribute the technology—that the other divisions had other specific applications important for our business success. I told him I appreciated his

feeling of ownership for the project, but I reminded him of our common goals. That helped smooth things over.

This case illustrates how the sponsor must understand and support the overall goals of the project.

*Effective sponsors focus on relating the change project to the broader goals of the organization.* Efforts in organizations can become dispersed. As people become deeply involved in their own programs, these programs sometimes take on a life of their own, separate from overall business strategies. The competent sponsor maintains support for change by repeatedly framing it in terms of *broader* organizational goals. "Why is training so important at this time?" asked one CEO. The human resource vice-president replied, "I'll tell you why; this business has to get done by *doing more with less.* That's our theme for this year. Anything that increases the competence of our people just a fraction is contributing to that."

*Skilled sponsors communicate why the change is needed to the total organization.* They *negotiate* for support by focusing on the most urgent needs of the organization, presenting concrete evidence that the change is essential for the organization's health and growth. They document basic reasons for management to be supportive of the change—cost effectiveness, time conservation, increased production, a competitive edge, or worker satisfaction. In technological projects, sponsors translate how technical interventions can produce practical results.

*Sponsors effectively utilize their power or status to overcome problems.*

## EXPECTING COOPERATION

One sponsor, a division general manager, described the following situation: "I was worried about our quality circles program. I started to hear rumblings. We weren't getting as many presentations as we had when it started, so I went to the person who was assigned the job of supervising to ask what was wrong. He said the circles were frustrated, because they couldn't get 'experts' from middle management to come and talk. I knew this was a familiar problem, so I went around for the next few days to meetings where I made it clear that I *expected* these managers to cooperate with quality circle efforts. I told them I expected results from them."

This judicious use of power is typical of effective sponsors. They understand where they have leverage, what interventions lend their support, and how to time their input for maximum effect. Likewise, the effective change team members know when to ask for the sponsor's help in overcoming obstacles.

*Sponsors "run interference" for the change team.* They buffer opposition and prejudice. Sometimes, when there is an ongoing need to run interference, the sponsor must assume both the role of manager and integrator.

*Sponsors continually update peers in higher management on change process steps.* This prevents obstacles from interfunctional or interdivisional rivalries. Most organizations with whom we consult are like tall chimneys where communications move up a division and arrive at the top. Sponsors prevent conflagrations by acting like a screen at the chimney tops, checking frequently to find out how the project is going, and having discussions with their colleagues from various divisions. In fact, effective sponsors find ways of influencing their colleagues to become *minisponsors* with their own coworkers.

*The key role of sponsors is to provide top management credibility and support for change projects.* They are the prime communicators to interpret how the change fits into the overall culture and vision of the organization. Sponsors are the prime negotiators for resources and the buffers who prevent and overcome opposition.

**To summarize:**

---

If your change effort needs a *sponsor,* look for someone who is good at
- Skillfully explaining the rationale for change and the steps necessary to bring it about,
- Using influence to obtain resources,
- Relating the change effort to the overall goals of the organization,

- Presenting concrete evidence that the change is essential for the health and growth of the organization,
- Utilizing personal power or status to overcome problems that occur during the change effort,
- Communicating to the broader organization why the change effort is necessary, and
- Continually *updating* peers in higher management on the steps taking place in the change process.

---

## THE POWER OF COMBINED EFFORTS

Individual contributions anchored in the six roles are essential to the life of the change project. It is their *combined efforts* that make innovation possible. It is not necessary for six distinct people to be involved. One person may play more than one role, but it is imperative that all six roles be covered.

Probably no area of management is more vital to change leaders than *appropriately* selecting and placing personnel for effective performance, fully utilizing strengths, and averting obvious weaknesses. The change leader's skill, balancing and coordinating the abilities and talents of everyone on the team, is critical for *effecting permanent change.*

Criteria for selecting the right people include: choosing persons for the roles honestly, selectively, and impartially; delegating responsibilities to role models to utilize fully their talents and skills; clarifying assignments and responsibilities, particularly when people assume multiple roles; avoiding conflicting role functions; confronting role vulnerabilities; and using the *total* human resources available.

## MAKE IT PERSONAL

The following questions can be used by a change leader for effective screening of candidates for the six roles. You may ask yourself the same questions when you wish to fill one of the team roles:

1.  In your opinion, which role do you most closely fit?

2.  Which qualities in that role do you most clearly demonstrate?

3.  If you were to use these qualities to the fullest, what would you alter in the change efforts in which you are now involved?

4.  Which qualities do you believe you could improve to make a *greater contribution* to the change effort?

5.  Do you feel you can function effectively assuming multiple roles?

6.  Can you think of people and resources you can utilize to help you fill the role you prefer?

7.  Is there some type of training or preparation that will help you to be more effective in the role you choose?

8.  What impact do you believe you can have on the specified change in the role you choose to fill?

# CHAPTER 6

# Implementing with Elegance

*Change leaders implement plans in discrete steps—clarifying initial intentions, ensuring acquisition of new skills, and refining change efforts to guarantee results.*

### GOOD IDEAS AREN'T ENOUGH

John, the senior vice-president for human resources at Universal Finance, was pleased. The first evaluations from participants of the training for the new performance appraisal system were good. There were the usual objections about all the paperwork interfering with real work, and other complaints, but nothing too startling. John reflected, "This is going to be easier than I thought. And we get to double-dip—a new performance appraisal system and a vehicle for solidifying our management-by-objectives program at the same time."

Universal Finance is one of the country's leading providers of financial services. Banking is its mainstay, but through a network of subsidiaries, Universal participates in as many types of financial services as the new, more liberal regulations permit. The chairman, a dynamic man, committed to change, had given John support for a new performance appraisal system, as long as he would assure implementation within a five-month period, tying it to the management-by-objectives initiative already in progress. John believed in piloting any significant new programs, so he made a simple plan that included starting the new system at corporate headquarters before sending it into the field. The staff at headquarters was a small group and he knew most of them. John thought he could get them to try out the system without a big risk of failure.

John was wrong! As with any change initiative, overlooked or unforeseen obstacles got in the way of effective implementation. First, a restructuring of corporate departments required rescheduling training for over 100 participants. John was already behind the timeline the chairman had set for him.

Next, the heads of corporate planning, marketing, and auditing each personally complained to him. After one of the training sessions, the head of planning told John, "It was a mess. My staff's saying we're totally unreasonable. They don't feel they have the kind of control over projects and milestones your system requires for getting rated well. They insist that when they service customers, they've got to react to what *the customer wants*—that's the objective—not what some appraisal system says they should be doing."

John responded, "Yes, of course you have to provide the best customer service. But, there's really not a conflict with the system. You should do both. They go hand-in-hand." John was on the defensive and wasn't going to listen. He didn't have time for *conflicts* between management-by-objectives and personal appraisal. He *had to* do both.

Blinded by the chairman's emphasis on objectives, John added training to the program. He had lost his focus and control of the project. Over the next few months, participants were almost literally "run" through the program to meet the deadline.

After five months, John had met his goal. Everyone had been trained in the new appraisal system and MBO. But, results were mixed at best. One participant, in evaluating his training wrote, "*Firehosed* with confusing material!" Another commented, "I'm not sure what the session was about, much less how I can use the material."

In any organization, people are its most valuable resource. Unfortunately, the introduction of "soft systems" to develop workers is notorious for generating reasonable ratings and few objective results.

The executives at Universal Finance had a good idea; they even had a specific plan based on sound management principles. However, John failed to cover the dimensions required for excellent implementation. His plans were not clear, particularly to key individuals from whom he needed support. He made a rudimentary attempt to incorporate the new appraisal system in stages, but was stymied by a poor choice of an initial group to pilot the system. Training, one of John's strengths, was instituted quite successfully. But ownership was a critical vulnerability in this implementation. Who owned the performance appraisal system at Universal—the chairman, who basically wanted it to be a covert extension of his management-by-objectives program; John, who envisioned a system that could unify and simplify the disparate—and sometimes unfair—forms of assessment performed throughout the company; or the managers who needed help in meeting their goals? Managers frequently resist programs focusing on performance development, feeling such programs usually are an extension of upper management control and an interference, not an aid, in getting the job done. John did not figure a way to generate quick, positive feedback about the system or develop a "pipeline" for assessing the relevance of his program, nor did he make ongoing revisions to fit end-user needs.

## I'M IN THE PROCESS OF CHANGING

Successful leaders make concrete plans. But, implementation is more than planning. It is a *process*. As the change effort evolves, the change leader must address a number of key issues to translate proposed actions into ongoing organizational practices.

As we outlined in Chapter 2, a set of *five key processes* support the process of successful implementations:

1. *Clarifying Plans*: A process in which implementors define, document, and specify the change.
2. *Integrating New Practices*: A process in which an organization incorporates change into its operations.
3. *Providing Education*: A process that fosters programs in which end users learn about and use new approaches and procedures.
4. *Fostering Ownership*: A process through which end users come to identify new processes and procedures as their own, rather than regarding them as changes imposed upon them.
5. *Giving and Getting Feedback*: A process in which a detailed objective is specified and input from the team is used to judge its effectiveness in the implementation plan.

In successful implementations, *the primary benefits of the change are made apparent to end users*. A major retail chain was having trouble reorganizing its warehouse systems. Managers had difficulty accepting the new systems until they and their supervisors toured the facilities of another company in another state that had instituted computerized inventory control. They were amazed at its efficiency and planned their own reorganization on the trip home.

Besides highlighting specific benefits of change *effective leaders also document the effects of implementation on the bottom-line in "hard" terms*. A manager of a chemical firm demanded pilot testing of a training program that documented results. He asked his trainers to be sure that changes in participants produced an objective business impact. Fortunately, the human resources personnel were able to quantify very significant improvement in job functioning in 4 out of 25 participants. They calculated the effect on operational efficiency and translated it into a projected dollar value. Even this small, tentative bottom-line result from additional training was enough to cost-justify an extensive program throughout a number of plants.

Sometimes unforeseen problems threaten change projects. One manager highlights the pitfalls of implementation:

> We rebuilt a set of integrated work stations in the basement. *Everybody* came to see them. We simulated a whole line and conducted training. The shop-floor management and the operators were really enthusiastic. Then we came in over the weekend to move the work stations upstairs to the plant itself. What a disaster! We couldn't move them onto the the freight elevator. It was so close, but they were one inch too high and two inches too wide. We spent the next month during the day disassembling and working nights reassembling the damn things. I guess I should have known *exactly* how big they'd be before we began!

## LET'S MAKE IT CLEAR

Change leaders begin *clarifying plans* early in the change effort. They determine if a plan is solid and workable by asking the following questions:

- Are *measurable* milestones and timelines built into the change plan?
- How *realistic* are the goals and time deadlines?
- What is the *specific* timeline for change?
- Why are the first group of end users selected?
- Are enough parts of the organization involved?
- Who is responsible for implementing the plan?

The initial form of the plan is only a start. All change plans require many revisions and an ongoing interpretation as the implementation progresses. Change leaders continue to *clarify* expectations about the implementataion just as they do when *preparing* their organization for change. Successful change leaders conduct an ongoing dialogue about each of the steps in their plans, with both their team and the end users.

Most organizations pay lip service to planning. We have found that over three quarters of change plans are unrealistic, or at best, problematic. For example, a project manager of an aerospace company put a gigantic PERT chart on his office wall. It covered an extensive space—at least 30 feet long—from ceiling to floor. When asked where was he on the "critical path," he replied, "Oh, we're completely off of it. The chart is no longer relevant, because top management changed their minds. I just haven't had time to take it down, because I'm so busy revising my plans." In most instances, it is better to have simple plans that specify how to overcome obstacles rather than technical plans that are unrealistic, as well as imposing, if not demoralizing. With a few simple initiatives, a leader can prevent the implementation of plans from becoming monumental.

*First, change leaders present a "preliminary plan" that outlines how to proceed through various implementation phases.* The preliminary plan should contain methods for winning support from individuals and the team about the *vital need to change;* reviewing *available* information about existing problems and defining missing data; *gathering and utilizing information; diagnosing problems* that exist or those that are likely to occur in the future; *solving potential problems,* employing best strategies for change; and subsequent *planning and goal-setting* that focuses on anchoring the change process to specific outcomes.

It is essential that the change leader present a specific plan. The clarity of the plan is the key to leading the change team into formulating goals and setting up procedures for achieving them. The most effecive leaders always *make initial plans simple.* The directives have to be reasonable and attainable. The steps inherent in the plan must be practical enough for end users to apply them immediately to their day-by-day activities. Most of all, the change leader must place primary importance on the current needs and demands of daily work tasks.

*Information-gathering* is a process that operates in every phase of the change implementation, but it must be an integral part of evolving a specific plan. Competent leaders most often conduct short, efficient, focused discussions with their coworkers to get vital information for designing a *relevant* plan. At an early stage, they involve the more influential members of the end-user group to participate in formulating the plan. For example, the leadership at Universal Finance did not invite key end users into the planning loop. Consequently some key user groups resisted implementation. In this and all other change efforts, group involvement and open dialogue produce a plan that reflects the relevant interests and concerns of end users.

*The change leader presents a written plan of action, with time-specific milestones that are clearly communicated to the organization.* Keep in mind, however, that written plans without people involvement may be misinterpreted. A director of a large government agency highlighted the problems inherent in communicating new plans:

> We tried having meetings, using visual aids to introduce our new plans, but without written documentation, the interpretations were muddled. Then I appointed a special staff member to write the plans for distribution. He was so taken with the importance of his assignment that he wrote reams and reams of directions. He even color-coded them in rainbow colors and the recipients spent so much time deciding which colored segment belonged to which activity that they became very confused and very angry. Then I tried another staff member and told her to be more direct and concise. Her communications were so brief that they had no substance. Finally, we realized we had to *involve a group* of people in formulating the plans and their presentation. The result was the plans were *relevant* to the group's specific needs. They understood them and they supported them."

*Change leaders make plans public.* Many organizations post written plans in a highly visible place and follow up with a procedure to ensure people participation. A multinational corporation used this method. The company was building a new facility that required moving about 50 percent of their employees from one location to merge with another 50 percent in another location. The "facilities committee" publicly posted a schedule with milestones and very specific details about what would happen to each group. They used a storyboard format, arranging the plans on cards pinned up on the wall of a centrally located office. Those affected could pin up other cards pointing out specific problems with each stage. This was done at each location with the facilities committee meeting at least once a week at the two sites to *discuss problems* and to *respond to the cards* of each group.

This case emphasizes the importance of both *publicizing the initial plan* and issuing *periodic accounts of progress* in executing the plan. Effective change leaders use both written communications and skillful meeting management to ensure the visibility of the plan. At intervals, they test to make sure they have a workable plan:

1. Is the plan concise and clearly written with *action steps*?
2. Is the written plan distributed to the *right personnel* to gain support?
3. Has the written plan had the *input* of an appropriate brainstorming group?
4. Have a number of *influential individuals* been interviewed to get their input?
5. Does the *style* of the written plan fit the organization?
6. Is *more than one method* employed to make the plan visible?
7. Is there both *a formal and informal network* to lend credence and support to the plan?

*The "plan communicator" usually has to be a top-notch public relations person* with the necessary skills to see that the initial planning stage is presented to the first end users without misinterpretation.

In addition to working for clarity, *change leaders assure that the change plan is realistic*. Practical plans contribute significantly to meeting critical milestones. The plan itself is a document for overcoming obstacles and personal stress. Sometimes anxious implementors skip milestones in order to keep "forward momentum" on the project. Most often *those* who skip a milestone will have to return to that point in the project and restart the process.

Change leaders can prevent planning from becoming a game of "Snakes and Ladders" by asking vital questions. Does the implementation plan lack clear milestones, outcomes, and deadlines? Are the timelines unrealistic? Is the responsibility for change plans unclear or unspecified? Leaders should review these three questions *repeatedly*, as they implement each step of the plan. Testing ensures that the plan is practical, acceptable to initial end users and effective in making a contribution to the overall change process. For instance, at Universal Finance, there was no specific evidence that the change plan was realistic or that it had been clarified and interpreted effectively enough to gain acceptance. The most signficant failure was that no one asked the critical questions to test the quality of their plans.

**To summarize:**

---

If *planning* is a problem in your change efforts
- Assign a responsible manager to the task of clarifying and interpreting plans.
- Make clear, specific plans:
  - Don't "skip" milestones.
  - Assign firm deadlines.
  - Define specific outcomes.
  - Publish and distribute the plans and practices, particularly to end users.
- Communicate day-to-day plans to ensure that the change has direction and movement.

---

## SLOW, BUT SURE

Organizations are not sponges with an infinite capacity for absorbing change. They need to *integrate new practices* gradually. One of the authors observed the consequences from not doing this when arriving very late one evening at a hotel in a small town. At the reception area, no staff members were in sight. Finally a harried receptionist appeared. She confirmed the reservation and gruffly produced a key. The author, being a sympathetic sort, asked her if anything was wrong. She burst out:

> Wrong! Look, when I came in last night, the management had installed this new computer and no one told me about it. It screwed up all the reservations. Just as I'm leaving, after I worked all night getting everything up-to-date again, I'm told my boss has been fired. I get home to find my husband is laid up and probably will be for the next six weeks. Then when I'm just getting up in the afternoon, I get a call telling me that the girl who fills in part-time during the evening hasn't shown up and could I come in? I come in and find that, during the day, they sold the hotel to someone else and we now have a new name and I think new bosses. How much change is one person expected to take?

This is the critical question for any organization. In 24 hours, most people do not face the amount of disruption experienced by the receptionist, but to assure successful adoption of new policies or practices, change leaders *gradually integrate* the change effort into an organization, gearing the rate of change to the organizational context, rather than cramming it into a prefixed timeline.

*Change leaders practice the "slow, but sure" approach to implementing change.* They prepare users for implementation and strive to make them as comfortable as possible about the innovation. Most managers hate this advice. One general manager told us, "If I had to wait for everyone to get comfortable about change, we would never change." Realistically, one cannot wait until *everyone* is comfortable, but following some simple procedures to assure that the change becomes integrated into the organization can help significantly. This process is something like decorating a house. Everyone wants their whole house decorated, but can't afford to leave the house while it's being done. Should the crew move every bit of furniture and strip every wall and get started on every room on the first day? Not if surviving the process is the goal. Instead, most homeowners proceed decorating one room at a time, so that they have some place to live in the meantime.

At Universal Finance their performance appraisal system was *instituted gradually,* a method consistent with successful change. Even in rapidly growing organizations, gradual implementation is the most effective method. A bank, implementing a new computer system, chose a small branch for initiating the change. Implementors picked this setting, because the branch manager was extremely supportive and the assistant manager—although superficially skeptical—was a real advocate when he believed in something. Carefully choosing the first setting for change and taking the time to get the buy-in of the branch manager and his assistant set the stage in the entire implementation process. Subsequently the bank staff used the first success to introduce the computer system in two more branches; then four, and finally, throughout the entire banking organization.

At Universal Finance, John, the key implementor, also chose only a selected segment of the corporate staff as the initial target for implementation. He saw the wisdom of using this group to interpret the new performance appraisal system to the entire corporation. However, since he failed to specify an encompassing vision, clear directions, and specific goals, his objective was not achieved.

With a small supportive group publicizing acceptance of an innovation, larger segments of the organization can be sold on change. It is human instinct to follow. Often those involved in the change projects ask, "Who's this worked for *up to now?*"

*Successful change leaders start the implementation with a few key users.* Many organizations institute massive changes by first involving a small group of end users, individuals who show spontaneous and unrestricted enthusiasm for the change. In introducing a new curriculum, one school administrator found that he could use a few teachers from his summer program to experiment with the curriculum in a more relaxed context. When the fall term began, he had them describe their summer success. At a meeting he arranged to present the new curriculum, he introduced the new approach and then asked for comments and opinions. The summer teachers, with genuine excitement, described their results—how the new methods of teaching saved time, stimulated the students more readily, and seemed more relevant to contemporay needs. Their support was more effective than any prescribed implementation the administrator could have initiated.

*Change leaders limit the amount of change introduced at one time.* This prevents the integration process from jarring and upsetting participants. Many successful change leaders have discovered that regulating the *speed* of the change process—slowing it down, if necessary, until acceptance and understanding is clear—produces more effective long-term results.

## MOVING DEPARTMENTS REQUIRES INTENSIVE CARE

One large hospital entered into a comprehensive building program that required the staff to retrain a segment of the support personnel. The senior hospital adminstrator and her staff worried about the disruption of services that might result if they moved all departments to the new building at the same time. Therefore, they decided to introduce a segment from three departments to the new building and its assets nine months before construction was completed. The director of personnel held meetings each month to train the group about the effects new equipment and architectural layout would have on their specific jobs. The upfront investment in time and resources helped participants gradually accept the change. One nurse summed it up, "The improvements sounded so good, I didn't mind walking through four different corridors to take my patients to occupational therapy." The administrator wisely slowed the speed of change. After the initial group had actually used some of the new facilities with success, the entire staff felt more confident about moving their departments.

*Change leaders start implementation with a "felt" need.* In starting a change effort, excellent leaders define *specific needs* of end users and continually focus on benefits to them. Leaders use the factors that cause tension, unrest, and intolerance or dissatisfaction as opportunities to point out the need for change. This helps participants see change as solutions to their problems rather than as new practices being externally imposed.

A computer systems designer for an insurance company told how he gained acceptance for his ideas: "I was taking the initial users through the CRT screens and they began looking very depressed. But I persisted. I kept reminding them about all the problems they had filling in the old forms, losing them, and having the claims adjustment department shout at them. They got the message."

*Change leaders publicize their change steps.* Not only must they share their *rationale* for the change, but they must also specify the procedures for change. As Disraeli said, "Man is so made . . . if he does not have an entire picture of a situation, he will latch on to the *fragments* and draw his conclusions from them." Change leaders have to enlarge the picture so end users can grasp the significance of the entire process—and not latch on to the fragments.

Competent change leaders publicize the initial steps of the integration process and employ methods of updating the organization on milestones and outcomes. In addition, they arrange for face-to-face feedback with influential individuals in both small and large groups. This kind of feedback makes the progress of change steps visible.

**To summarize:**

---

If you are having problems with *integrating new practices*
- Prepare for the change:
  - Ensure that the rationale and procedures for change are well known.
  - Describe the change in end users' terms.
- Limit the amount of change introduced in any one phase of the implementation:

- Pilot the change with a limited group.
- Introduce the change in small steps with specific milestones.
- Integrate change steps with a high probability of success.
• Enlist firm support for change:
  - Select end users with a commitment or vested interest in the change.
  - Seek allies for support.

---

## LEARNING TO CHANGE

Successful organizations use a variety of techniques for *providing education.* Average implementors often offer training, but do not invest the same resources or utilize as many principles of adult education as their more successful counterparts.

Managers often decry the expense and allocation of time required for excellent training. However, poor teaching leads to poor retention and little or no real skill acquisition. Most total failures in planned change can be linked to little or no training. Less successful implementors tend to use only one method of training—lecture followed by some sort of practice and discussions that tend to be technical in nature. One trainer reported, "We have a lot of material to cover, so we've got to move fast. You know you can't meet everybody's needs. Most people get it in the end." In contrast, the most successful programs meet *everyone's needs.*

*Change leaders provide education as an integral part of the implementation process.* They foster programs to help end users learn about the *nature* and *use* of all new procedures. Without training, excellent new programs can fail. Poor attitudes and prejudices may persist. Vital knowledge and skills remain unlearned. The publisher of a progressive newspaper, in introducing a number of innovative policies, called his staff together and announced: "We tend to *oppose* that which *we do not understand* . . . for that reason, we expect to spend an inordinate amount of time helping you *understand* these new policies, before we implement them."

Outside consultants and resource people can sometimes add credibility to educational programs, stimulating in-house groups to accept new approaches. Inside experts usually can clarify specialized aspects of the change that connect with overall organizational objectives.

*Change leaders use good training to protect the investment an organization has in new procedures and processes.* For example, Universal protected its new performance appraisal system with a vigorous training program. In another example, an advertising agency tried to improve the productivity of copy writers by teaching them word processing for generating original text. However, the agency provided only instructional manuals and no formal training, assuming that the copy writers were "smart people" and could figure out the details for themselves. For the first six months, only half of the copy writers used their PCs. Training classes helped the copy writers discover how much time they could save and how fast they could turn out finished copy using personal computers. In a follow-up assessment of the change project, one hundred percent of the writers were word processing their copy.

*Change leaders relate training to the basic needs of the end user.* Clever trainers, recognizing that *interpretation* is a necessary part of accepting innovation, find effective ways to "sell" how new procedures and practices help end users with their everyday needs. A firm, introducing a new telephone system, began a training course by having the participants list *everything* they do with the telephone. After a group discussion, the trainer showed how each of the items mentioned by the group worked on the new system. The trainer then asked the group to brainstorm about any additional uses they could imagine for the telephone. About a quarter of these were possible with the new system. The company estimated that by employing this method, participants used more than twice the number of features following training than the participants in other telephone system implementations.

*Change leaders ensure the relevance of the educational experience.* One of the most effective methods for evaluating relevance is to interview participants about the training. Some questions for assessing the effectiveness of training include:

1. Is the specific training program helping you understand how to integrate the change?
2. Is the training geared to your present work procedures and tasks?
3. Is it relevant to your current problems and concerns?
4. Is it stimulating enough to motivate you to want to change?
5. Is it easy to understand, simply expressed, and free of ambiguities?
6. Does it give you new insight and encourage you to explore further?
7. Is it open-ended with the promise of offering you additional growth as you understand more?

Written feedback can be very useful too, particularly if leaders need to evaluate strengths and weaknesses of teaching to a large group of participants.

*Change leaders use a variety of educational techniques.* They invest time to assess, pilot, and refine the very best meeting techniques, presentation skills, and adult education practices. For example, adult learning relies on the prior experiences of end users. It assumes that the knowledge and training participants already have are pertinent. The focus, then, is on refinement and application. This requires time for reflection as well as activities and a recognition that people learn in different ways. As a result, the best training efforts match methods with the style and experience of the audience. Teaching occurs in a range of group participation activities—brainstorming, role playing, interviewing, task force input, and open discussions. This taps into all learning styles and keeps interest high.

In today's world with media presentations available at every turn, it has become increasingly important for teachers, presenters, and change leaders to become master presenters. They should *cultivate a professional presentation image.* If they are not skilled presenters, they can practice, seek coaching or formal training, or use coworkers or outside personnel to make presentations that ensure the message gets across. For example, a manager of personnel for a large corporation who was a master politician always polished his presentations to include relevant data and to address all possible political considerations. Unfortunately, he was an insufferable bore to his audience, because he didn't meet their *listening and learning* needs. In this case, the manager improved his skills through coaching to help him apply some simple techniques for entertaining and motivating and interacting with audiences.

*Change leaders create a climate in which end users seek self-improvement.* They challenge end users *to learn more, to make new contributions,* and *to improve* the quality of performance. These challenges ensure that educational programs modify behavior, change production, and produce insight. If educational programs are well conceived, end users will expand their knowledge and skills and support the change team's training efforts.

*Change leaders offer a thorough educational process about the change.* A simple story about an operational change illustrates the importance of *providing education* for an innovation. When an entire office was computerized and each person in the office was introduced to several new machines, an imaginative office manager invited two technical experts from an outside source to spend five days with the staff. Each morning the experts began the day with a stimulating meeting, employing all kinds of visuals to dramatize the use of the machines. Over coffee, they conducted an open discussion, followed by questions. The day was filled with an abundance of hands-on training and individual coaching and tutoring. At the end of each day, group members came together again for further questions and formulated a written evaluation of what they had experienced. The two trainer-experts spent time each evening picking up cues from the evaluations to plan the next day's instruction. The hands-on training built the confidence of the workers. The interaction with the group built a climate for acceptance. They gained an understanding specific to their setting that made them want to change.

Often leaders view training in a limited manner. The most successful change projects and programs employ a range of methods for teaching and motivating, including formal hands-on education and training on a regular basis and orientations directed at the initial end users first. An expanded program of education is offered to a broader sphere of the organization, using the initial end users in a group process. In sessions, courses, and workshops trainers employ adult education procedures, such as brainstorming, role-playing, group discussion techniques, and panel presentations. Task forces teach through problem-solving around special tasks and isolated issues. Newsletters, bulletins, and other written communications, such as monographs or self-study packages teach, inform, and educate. Visuals of all forms—films, videos, transparencies, and various graphics—reinforce the teaching of new procedures and concepts. Frequent use of training evaluations in written form, as well as personal interviews with those trained, help judge training and improve on future programs. The goal for every training effort is to make learning fun and effective. This requires variety and a real concern, not only for the objectives of training, but also for the learning needs of participants.

**To summarize:**

---

If you have problems *providing education*
- Formulate programs that specify the key principles underlying the changes in operation.
- Clarify the objectives of training:
  - Ask end users what skills and knowledge they need to implement change.
  - Incorporate end users' suggestions and language into the teaching program.
- Design training that results in job-related skills:
  - Provide opportunities for hands-on practice.
  - Make training relevant to day-to-day work.
  - Involve participants in self-directed exercises.
  - Customize the length and type of training to each group of end users.
- First, start training with motivated or influential end users.
- Evaluate the effects of training:
  - Observe work practices.
  - Obtain end-user feedback about the effectiveness of training, and incorporate suggestions in future programs.

---

## NOW IT'S MINE

If prepared properly, any organization will see change as desirable. However, the change leader still must *foster ownership* of the project. Too many managers believe resistance will evaporate in the natural process of change. But, what is the cost?

*Change leaders empower employees to make change happen.* They pass the baton to employees in a way that enables them to tap the inner resources of employees. Once end users feel they are included and involved in all of the moves of implementation—plans, decisions, and outcomes—they develop a sense of *ownership* in the entire change effort. When they *understand* and *participate,* they become *committed* to current and future strategies and directives.

Who owns the Universal Finance performance appraisal system and why? Clearly there is a level of support from top management. But, do Universal's managers feel that the system is helping them or do they feel that they will have even more forms to complete? Most often, resistance builds when these systems are not seen as *helping* the manager. Instead, they are perceived as corporate routines to tolerate or as a means of control over some aspect of the manager's life.

*Change leaders know that people support systems they perceive as personally helpful to them.* When effective change leaders implement programs, they focus on the *needs* of the users. An executive of a company that was successful in implementing a performance improvement system had her managers rank order all the things about performance that they wanted to modify. By confronting their top concerns, managers became more deeply involved in the whole change process.

A middle-level manager who had been very skeptical of quality circles was converted—and even became a facilitator—when one circle solved a crucial problem that was under his jurisdiction. He admitted:

> I never thought quality circles could solve such a severe problem. After all, I have had six years of chemistry and chemical engineering training and I thought I was on top of it! But, I *saw* the quality circle

do the job. I thought it was just going to be a 'touchy-feely' pain in the ass. I was dead wrong."

*Change leaders build in incentives for using the new policies, practices, or processes.* For some people, simple, objective feedback is enough to reinforce the change. As part of a factory automation project, terminals were placed on the shop floor to give foremen accurate data about the rates at which their machines were running. In turn, the foremen taught their operators how to obtain the data and what it meant. After nine months, operator morale increased, output was higher and wastage lower than projected for the change. In contrast, at a similar plant, the terminals were locked up for fear of sabotage. The implementation process was very slow and the effects on productivity were limited. Operator morale decreased considerably, because the operators perceived the terminals as a method for controlling them.

*Change leaders involve others and utilize others' talents and skills in every phase of the implementation.* They practice participative management, fostering ownership by developing and using the creativity and energy of workers. This requires a deft balance between control and facilitation; formal and informal discussions; recognition of individual and group efforts; loosely fashioned strategies and firmly committed plans.

Too often organizations demand change by legislating programmatic steps. Mostly, this is just substituting one form of paternalism for another. Effective change occurs when leaders make certain that *structure* will create rather than inhibit innovation.

*Change leaders unleash the power in the group by sponsoring personal opinions and growth.* They tolerate and promote the formation of informal communication links, new relationships and conditions that cut across traditional organizational structures. In addition, they encourage the development of new roles and new formal and informal teams. Most of all, they allow ideas of the group to evolve, mistakes to be made, and plans to be revised.

*Change leaders stay in touch with end users' daily tasks.* Once end users are convinced that a change will help them control and improve their daily tasks, they join forces with implementors.

This happened in a large manufacturing firm when the product research group advised changing the kind of material used in manufacturing large steam turbines. The change involved using steel instead of copper for one small engine part. To outsiders, the change was insignificant, but to insiders, it was heresy. One worker protested: "We've always used copper; steel might not work. Why take a chance?" Product research had documented that this change would be more cost effective and would eliminate the problem of long waits for the delivery of copper, since steel was more readily available. The initial attempt to "sell" the end users failed. Two years later, a new manager involved the end users in plans by asking their advice for assuring availability of materials. He held a series of 70-minute morning meetings for a month and shared all of the research data with them. He had a financial expert to come in to explain cost effectiveness. By keeping discussions focused on basic manufacturing needs, the manager was able to convince the end users that they would *personally* benefit from the change to steel. Not only would it eliminate the wait for copper, but with a cost-effective program in the division, their chances of raises would increase.

*Successful change leaders foster involvement to give end users a feeling of ownership.* Because end users are on the firing line every day, they can make important contributions to the change effort. A number of organizations have had the insight to *offer special incentives* to end users for new ideas. For example, many of the Fortune 500 companies use an array of contests, cash awards, bonus incentives, and pay raises as carrots for innovation.

Workers often "invent" new products when they are in settings that encourage initiative. In fact, our studies indicate that more new products and procedures come from the ordinary worker than from top management, when opportunities for ingenuity and exploration are sponsored. In the most innovative organizations, managers always *honor, respect,* and *reward* the creativity of coworkers.

*Change leaders are excellent delegators.* Many told us that they became very good at anticipating and averting problems, but that they failed to *empower* end users and team members. They became so involved in launching plans that they failed to *trust* others. We frequently heard comments, such as, "I'm not sure my team is ready to take over." This resulted in an unhealthy paternalism—keeping too many ideas and activities under close scrutiny. One manager clearly described how he stopped undermining his subordinates and made his own life easier too:

> I was exhausted carrying the whole burden. I even thought I had an ulcer, I was getting so many stomachaches. One morning I woke up and realized I had to pass some of the responsibilities to the team . . . the minute I did that, making the change stopped being such a struggle. In fact, it became an exciting adventure, not just for me, but for the whole team."

When leaders foster ownership, they not only have to anticipate problems, but they have to give plausible directions for solving problems. They become involved on a daily basis with end users to direct problem-solving strategies that contribute to change processes.

**To summarize:**

---

If you have problems *fostering ownership*
- Plan change in ways that benefit end users:
  - Increase end users' control over job tasks.
  - Enhance end users' roles.
  - Frame the change in a manner that increases the end users' self-image or status in the organization.
  - Ensure quick, visible benefits.
- Involve end users in the change process:
  - Ask for suggestions before implementation; use end users as consultants.
  - Specify "milestones" for seeking end-user feedback.
  - Institute special methods (e.g., meetings, surveys, feedback sheets) for specifying feedback.
  - Publicize ways in which user suggestions are incorporated in change plans.

- Build in incentives for innovation and change.
- Collaborate with end users about ways to integrate changes into normal operations.

---

## GIVING AND GETTING FEEDBACK

The change leader needs *feedback* to determine the impact of the change and to refine the steps of implementation. Effective leaders employ a rich spectrum of feedback methods—face-to-face encounters, written communications, interviews with end users for their ideas and suggestions, task forces, working committees, and suggestion boxes.

*Change leaders generate feedback during each step in the change process.* First, they document and describe the *expected* outcomes of the change. Then, they obtain feedback immediately after the implementation.

In well-executed efforts, significant benefits of the change occur very soon after initial implementation. For example, our research in quality circles revealed that if a circle was able to solve a problem, of whatever size, within *the first three months* of its existence, it was more likely to confront a major issue in its first year. Furthermore, circles that did this lasted longer than circles that did not have an early success.

As the change implementation progresses, effective leaders track milestones as the team reaches them, and acknowledge key successes. By "getting down in the trenches" with coworkers, leaders can encourage them to focus on the importance of each step in the change process, lead them to define problems, and generate possible solutions.

*Change leaders also use a variety of feedback tools tailored to their settings and personnel. Direct observations* include both verbal and nonverbal cues. Many are behavioral and require interpretation with more than a hit and miss procedure. Keen perception and insight are essential for this kind of feedback. Some leaders have found they improved their observation skills by holding individual interviews. One leader stated, "I became better at picking up behavioral cues the more I arranged personal interviews. At first, I overlooked some of the obvious cues, but with practice, I became a lot more perceptive. I got so I could really 'read' people even in informal talks on the shop floor."

Most management teams require some type of *written reports* that reflect daily or weekly activities. However, one CEO we interviewed highlighted the basic truth about reports:

> No type of report has been invented that will give you the whole picture . . . people are going to make themselves look as good as possible on a report form. . . . It is still necessary to devise other means of feedback to be sure you do not miss the essentials. . . . I do think reports serve a purpose—they can *verify* your instincts, observations, and information that comes in from other sources.

Managers use *responses,* which usually are answers to specific memos or inquiries. As opposed to reports that are more routine, leaders usually solicit these for special purposes. They can be verbal or written.

*Brainstorming or group feedback* comes from bringing together a specific group to evaluate, react, and discuss conditions in specific ways. This kind of group process can provide excellent feedback, if a leader gives members of the group freedom to be honest, straightforward, and direct.

*Change leaders make giving and getting feedback a habit.* One participant in a change project confessed, "I don't pay much attention to all that 'feedback' stuff, because I don't see anybody paying much attention to what we say." This can kill an implementation. End users must see change leaders *using and relying* on their feedback. Not only must leaders show appreciation for input, but they also must ensure they will modify the implementation as a result of it.

Since most people are invested in hiding their true feelings—especially in the company of influential executives—change leaders must continually press for effective feedback. They check the "grapevine" and other informal groups, such as "coffee clutches" and informal gatherings around the water-cooler. The information change leaders gain from these informal sources is often more useful than any formal procedure.

One manager described the payoff from fostering ongoing feedback, "I learned that you have to use *many* devices to get at the truth. People have different settings where they tell what they think. You've got to make someone feel that they aren't at risk. Then, sooner or later, they reveal their true feelings."

*Change leaders share feedback, not only with end users, but with the entire organization.* When individuals see that others share their views, they gain confidence to speak out more often about their true opinions. To help the entire organization have a total picture of what is happening, effective change leaders publicize both problems and progress, elicited through written and verbal feedback. This is an investment in the future. By sharing information openly, change leaders generate *team spirit* and *commitment* to present and future implementation goals.

**To summarize:**

---

If you have problems with *giving and getting feedback*
- Institute high visibility or high impact changes first.
- Use a range of feedback processes.
- Make sure project outcomes are clear, accessible, rewarding, and relevant.
- Ensure that the process of feedback includes the larger organization.
- Utilize feedback to advance the change effort.
- Publicize that you are using coworkers' suggestions and input.

---

## PUTTING IT ALL TOGETHER

To accomplish all five processes of the implementation, leaders use all of the competencies they have learned about change. To achieve excellent results, they cultivate the most polished attributes of a change leader, they select the most skilled team to implement the change, and they define and refine a workable plan. Most of all, change leaders recognize that they have the primary responsibility of *coordinating* all five of the implementation processes.

## MAKE IT PERSONAL

Since implementation is a process requiring an evolving set of responses and strategies, at intervals ask the following questions to keep your planned change on track.

1.  Is my plan specific enough?

2.  Am I communicating goals and milestones and specifying tasks?

3.  Have I provided for clarifying the plan at each step of the implementation?

4.  Have I arranged for an ongoing program of education about the change?

5.  Am I using the best skills and talents available in the organization?

6.  Have I monitored the performance of those filling the change team roles?

7.  Am I influencing others to get adequate buy-in?

8.  Am I negotiating and compromising to attain the overall goals of the change effort?

9.  Are we reaching milestones and am I rewarding the team for achieving milestones and goals?

10. Do my coworkers identify with the new processes and procedures as their own?

11. Have I consistently asked my team for feedback and suggestions?

12. Have I publicized how we are using the team's input?

# PART III

# MAKING ORGANIZATIONAL CHANGE HAPPEN

| CHAPTER 7

# Making Change Work

*Effective leaders employ planning throughout the
course of purposeful change, using the best
change leadership practices to guide the process.*

## SIMPLE STEPS

All successful change plans are revised many times over the
course of implementation. As the change process unfolds,
effective leaders must incorporate new strategies to confront
vulnerabilities and human factors that emerge with each stage,
and to maintain momentum in the change effort. The past
three chapters have described the specific practices that un-
derlie change leadership. The three-part model presented
helps change leaders *prepare* their organizations for change,
*choose the right people* for effective teamwork, and *implement the
right interventions* to produce visible results. This chapter focuses on methods of planning—on the ways that leaders incorporate the best practices into organized action, steps that
produce results.

Change leaders are proactive planners. They use repeated
planning as an active method for refining activities and produc-

ing results. First of all, they frame *preliminary plans* to launch the change process and test the feasibility of early proposals. In the initial phase of a change project, plans are more *a set of directions* to point the way for progress—a beginning road map. These preliminary directions stimulate discussion with coworkers, preparing them for collaborative efforts. Early plans also serve as a document for clarifying ideas and uncovering inconsistencies. The detailed landmarks of the change journey are specified only later in more advanced, expanded iterations of change plans.

In practice, change efforts fail for two primary reasons—not *knowing* the right interventions or not *implementing* the right interventions. A middle manager at a computer software company highlights the problem with implementing innovations, "I know what has to get done and I know the basic steps for getting it done. That's the easy part. But, when your boss changes deadlines and your staff makes mistakes or gets flaky, your plans go to hell. That's the hard part—getting things back on track and keeping them there." Another manager of a factory automation project clarifies an additional problem with planning:

> The hard thing about making a change is that it's new. You don't have a proven method outlining how to get it done, so you've got to be *very organized* and *very specific* and *very persistent.* Everyone thinks that innovation is some kind of magic—you wave a wand, Lee Iaccoca walks by, and your robots are up and running. Mostly, you succeed by slogging through the details and overcoming misjudgments and mistakes. You've got to handle the change *in small steps* so that you don't get lost.

The small steps necessary for handling change are the essential *content* of the plan. In simple terms, a project plan evolves over time to reflect each phase of management interventions, as Figure 7-1 shows.

Just as the plan is a vehicle for completing each phase, the phases are the *vehicles* for completing the entire *process* of the change effort. In addition, change leaders infuse each phase

**Figure 7-1.   Management Steps in the Change Process.**

| Change Definition | Objective |
|---|---|
| ⬇ | ⬇ |
| Information Gathering | Concerns and Resources |
| ⬇ | ⬇ |
| Organizational Diagnosis | Strategies |
| ⬇ | ⬇ |
| Problem Solving | Goals |
| ⬇ | ⬇ |
| Action Planning | Master Plan |

with a special set of interventions. In its totality, the process we have described is the *vehicle* for developing and refining the *content* or *specific actions, resources,* and *responsibilities* that make each plan iterative and its steps into a cohesive, effective whole. It is the glue for holding together the change process.

### Phase 1: Change Definition— Where Were You? Where Are You Now? Where Are You Going? And How Will You Get There?

*Effective change leaders define proposed changes in detail.* Every new direction needs a focus; every specific plan depends on how individuals in the organization perceive the new system, process, or procedure. A leader clarifies the steps in the plan and creates a preliminary road map. Even though the plan will inevitably undergo many revisions in subsequent phases of implementation, there has to be a clearly communicated starting point.

*Competent leaders set the pace for change* by specifying, clarifying, and supporting implementation goals. When they specify *what* to change and *how*, they avoid false starts and wasted effort. Members of an advanced technology group were asked by their corporate leadership to accelerate automation in one of its businesses. The technical specialists became increasingly frustrated, because they received limited support. The management team, although manifestly in favor of the technology, was ambivalent about the role of advanced technologies in their business. One senior technologist complained, "Every time we go to top management, it seems the ground rules have changed. We bring in a justification for increasing inventory turnover. We get told that inventory turnover is no longer important. We bring in a justification for improved material specs and they tell us to look at its impact on market share. Sometimes we feel we can't win." The ambivalence of top managers diffused the focus on new technologies. As a result, nothing happened. Several years later, management changed. The new leadership *specified a plan* and a clear set of expected outcomes—cost reductions from design through production, faster product introductions, and better integration between design and manufacturing. With a clearer direction and consistent support, the technology group developed one of the show pieces for automated manufacturing.

## Phase 2: Information Gathering— I'm Open to Suggestions

Information gathering supports all the phases of change projects. *Effective change leaders perform significant "upfront" information gathering* and continue exploring options throughout the change effort. They spend considerable amounts of time gathering data before formulating their agenda. For example, the manager at a large industrial company felt that the design and quality of a major product line was deficient. Before making a commitment to the next generation of products, he developed a "want" list for how their products should perform and how they should look by asking those who buy, sell, service, and manufacture them. He received over 1,000 serious suggestions; more than 700 of them were incorporated into the design of the next product line.

Information gathering and idea testing highlight both the vulnerabilities of the organization and its key resources before leaders make major commitments to the change process. Inquiry can take a number of forms. One effective method is to arrange for feedback from those most affected by the change. A manufacturer of equipment for utilities and other similar industries anticipated a change in market demand. As they began to formulate a plan, top management worried, not only about what actions they should take, but also about the effect of change on the immediate performance of their employees. If production slowed or proved unable to meet the new market demand, they would be trading one problem for another—a production deficit versus noncompetitive products. Meanwhile, rumors of an imminent change mushroomed out of control. Management asked a consultant from corporate headquarters for help. He closeted himself in a room with a flip chart and asked people to visit him and discuss their concerns about the change. The consultant papered the walls with their worries. With his help, top management defined the main themes and developed strategies for answering concerns. Their summary became a road map for communication efforts. By including workers' suggestions in their plans, they decreased resistance to change and developed a more effective strategy for meeting potential production demands. Because their information-gathering effort was so successful, they began to employ similar methods to generate ideas and test possibilities for future plans. In this case, a significant success actually became part of the practice and culture of the company.

Another effective method for gathering information entails *assessing employee and management attitudes and practices.* Leaders gather a variety of opinions from colleagues and end users, from managers of other sections in the business, and even those outside the organization who use its products or services. The broad perspective gained from multiple inputs that include various business functions and customers often generate ideas for more practical, effective change efforts.

Information-gathering also serves another function. It can clarify specific ways coworkers can help change leaders accomplish their initiatives. One manager discussed what he did before introducing a new piece of manufacturing equipment to his operation:

> I realized that the operators saw me as the "new kid on the block," but I needed their help in getting the equipment going. I spent the first week casually talking to the foreman on the day shift. Gradually I gained his confidence. Then, I told him about my idea of bringing in a new piece of equipment that would speed production. He was quite enthusiastic. I leveled with him, "I'm going to need your help in two areas—finding out exactly how this equipment is going to affect the way you do your job in the plant and selling it to the operators." He was one step ahead of me. He reeled off several suggestions that assured my success."

Information gathering can also surface conflicts. By obtaining opinions and testing ideas openly, change leaders help clarify perceptions and confront conflicts among various organizational groups. For example, a large manufacturing firm started a change effort that entailed consolidating two manufacturing plants into one. Top management perceived the change as a competitive necessity for the survival of the business. Line managers and workers saw themselves being phased out of a job. The result was widespread demoralization—even some sabotage. After several missed milestones, the project leader started a series of discussions to clarify the problems. The extent and nature of job cutbacks was specified and the need for change was presented. By dispelling some of the unfounded fears, the project proceeded on schedule.

## Phase 3: Diagnosis— What's in Our Way?

*Top change leaders are masterful at defining barriers to innovation.* All too often, vital vulnerabilities are left unattended, while energy is directed toward other issues. This became apparent in a recent culture change project. The CEO of an aerospace company wanted to bring about change in the "people management" side of his business. He felt that "traditional" approaches to management, which he equated with Theory X approaches, would not be appropriate to manage today's work force or to drive the types of strategic changes he felt the company required to meet future challenges. Top management spent considerable time listening to "people management gurus." However, an attitude study, administered throughout the company, revealed that the real "management culture" problem was not so much the Theory X issue ("all stick and no carrot management"), but a deficit of *delegation*. Even the top managers engaged in extensive technical problem-solving. This policy was not conducive to retaining and developing young engineers, since they were given very little responsibility and little opportunity to develop vital engineering skills. The culture change project was eventually redirected to focus more sharply on what managers had to do to develop and retain their people, including a specific training program in delegation.

*"People" problems derail change efforts far more often than technical or procedural problems.* All too often, the major focus of a change effort is on the technical and mechanical aspects of the change, ignoring interpersonal and team conflicts that inevitably influence all planned change. One effective technique for defining these barriers is to perform a *people audit*. For example, one leader described how he had his change team *diagnose* potential problems with their coworkers. "We took a piece of paper and listed those people who would be most supportive on one side; on the other side, we listed those who would be most resistant. On another sheet, we listed all the reasons *why* the supportive people would support change, and on the opposite side, all the reasons *why* resistant workers would be resistant. Then we discussed how to increase the positive reasons. For instance, demonstrating to the salespeople specific ways the system will really help them. And we discussed how to decrease the negative reasons. For example, we talked about planning a training program to educate the group about the merits of the change. Finally, we formulated a plan for decreasing organizational and human barriers." Using this kind of approach, particularly in a dialogue with coworkers, can help leaders generate effective strategies and a group of *active partners* in change.

All barriers to change are not equally important to confront. Furthermore, barriers to change are often deeply imbedded in stubborn, long-standing attitudes and practices. Therefore, trying to resolve too many problems can prove impossible, if not destructive. The best leaders instinctively focus on problems that have *very significant costs* to the organization, if ignored, and concentrate on factors that have the *most positive leverage* on the business. In some settings the positive factors might be quality or productivity; in others, it might be worker satisfaction or quality of work life.

Setting priorities about which barriers to confront requires that change leaders devise ways of avoiding emotional pitfalls. Most often, priorities can be clarified in discussions that try what-if simulations for the various vulnerabilities defined as problems. Leaders gain vital credibility from colleagues by demonstrating a willingness to confront issues in open dialogue. These discussions should focus initially on a *visible* barrier to change. Best leaders not only confront high-visibility, high-cost barriers, but also focus on problems for which they have available resources. No matter what the focus, change leaders help the team concentrate on issues, strategies, and objective concerns, not personalities. They avoid getting entangled in inevitable personality differences and conflicts. Although the major goal of leaders is planned change, using group process methods also promotes individual and team development.

## Phase 4: Problem-Solving— Vulnerabilities as Strategies

*Effective change leaders continually solve problems and reframe vulnerabilities into opportunties.* Problem-solving is a process that requires openness, creativity, and flexibility. For example, an engineering manager wanted to design a new product quickly. He challenged his team to tell him all the reasons it couldn't be done. After they listed the reasons, he told his team, "Eliminating these barriers is our road map for what we've got to do to quickly design the new product in time to meet the competition." He then assigned responsible people to solve each problem listed by the team. Their commitment to being problem solvers motivated them to complete the assignment quickly and effectively.

Problem-solving starts the moment leaders decide which organizational barriers to confront and continues during each subsequent step in the change process. The best leaders enact timely interventions to build and maintain momentum. Although goal-setting, planning, feedback, and plan revision are separate tasks, each one relies on effective problem-solving techniques. When vulnerabilities require problem-solving efforts, follow the practices outlined in Chapters 4-6. By directly fostering these practices, you speed up the process of confronting obstacles. By considering a variety of solutions, and by obtaining suggestions from others, particularly the people who have to live with the change, leaders can tailor solutions to their organizations. In practice, the best problem-solving efforts encompass both the reality of "today's actual situation" and the ideal of "what the situation should be." The best leaders help their teams define and reduce the gaps between the reality of their situations and the ideals they wish to attain.

## Phase 5: Strategy and Action-Planning— Putting Together the Pieces

*Change projects often fail from lack of focus or steps that are poorly defined or too difficult to implement.* Quality action-planning results from organizing team efforts into small, discrete activities. Leaders accomplish this by starting with the *outcomes* they want. Next, they define the *goals* necessary to achieve them and finally specify the *action steps* the team must perform to reach the goals.

The most critical skill to learn is goal-setting.

*Well-defined goals are a prerequisite for productive actions.* Merely the act of setting goals increases the probability for goal completion and overall productivity. However, competent change leaders fashion high-impact goals that are *relevant, specific, realistic and attainable,* and *measurable.*

*Specific* goals employ a single behavior, number, unit of time, and so on. The desire to produce the best incentive scheme is too general and "fuzzy," but increasing entrepreneurial activity through the generation of a specific level of new sales in a particular time frame is specific enough to contribute to the improvement of an organization's performance.

*Realistic* goals are those that are *possible to achieve* with the available talent and resources. They should not be an arbitrary "pie in the sky" activity. Goals of this kind are not infrequent. For example, the leader of a software project asked each team member to assess how long his or her set of tasks would "realistically" take. The leader added the time for the cumulative tasks and found they were going to require *twice* the time she had been given to meet her deadline. So, she made up a project flow chart about tasks and milestones in which she divided everybody's estimates by *two!* One member of the team captured the team's attitude: "This is bull—it's so ridiculous and so typical, I'm just going to work at my own pace. That's all I can do, since no one pays attention to reality."

In contrast, goals should not be so simple to accomplish that little or no effort is required to meet them. Unchallenging goals breed complacency and waste talent.

*Measurable* goals are those that are concrete enough to generate specific data. This information is valuable for following accomplishments and generating feedback about problems and potential solutions.

Leaders must set different kinds of goals during each phase of the change process. In the initial phases of planned change, they must balance the need for direction against the anxiety and premature closure that result from rigid goal-setting and overspecified plans. To strike this balance, effective leaders set broad performance goals in early phases of change. They define the scope and scale of the change effort, but not the specific strategies, timelines, milestones, or activities. The initial performance goals specify the outcome the change leaders envision and provide an agenda for starting a dialogue among collaborators. As the change effort progresses, new types of goals are required—specific goals with short timelines, covering only a single phase of change to assure their completion.

What is the best way to begin the goal-setting process? It usually begins with information gathering, diagnosis, and problem-solving. During these stages, change leaders ask, "What results do I want?" After defining a best outcome, they ask, "What objective measures or accomplishments represent an *excellent* result?" Next, leaders take time to improve goals through simplifying, objectifying, and testing them to assure that they confront the most significant barriers to change.

The most important questions for assuring the quality of goals include

- Are the goals easy to understand? Simply expressed?
- Are they results oriented; not activity oriented?
- Are they limited in number and scope?
- Are they specific in their description of qualities, quantities, responsible people, constraints, and costs?
- Are they timebound with specific deadlines and milestones?
- Are they challenging?
- Are they designed for measurement and feedback?

*Well-defined goals are a prerequisite for productive activities.* However, they focus on one aspect of a plan only—clear outcomes. They must be incorporated into a more comprehensive framework, called *an action plan,* to be truly effective.

*An action plan* is a contract for change. It should include specific outcomes and clear goals, plan steps or tasks, responsible people, milestones, and deadines. Figure 7-2 shows the chart for a master plan.

A simple plan, however, only represents a set of possibilities. It requires skilled leadership for implementation. Four general leadership skills support the master plan. They include

1. *Utilizing* and *customizing* the strategies related to organizational readiness, team development, and areas of implementation;
2. Employing specific *planning skills,* such as *goal-setting* (i.e., specifying objectives, responsible people, and other resources);

**Figure 7-2.   A Master Plan.**

| GOALS | PLAN PRIORITIES | IMPLEMENTORS | DESIRED OUTCOME |
|-------|-----------------|--------------|-----------------|
| Overall objectives | Defined Tasks | Responsible People: | Results with Time Frames: |

3. Using professional *communication and presentation skills* (i.e., effective meetings and a well-presented, clearly written plan); and

4. *Refining influence skills* to assign tasks, give direction, foster accountability, monitor desired outcomes, and motivate workers.

Even well-documented plans supported by effective leadership can fail. Most often, this occurs when personal and organizational factors are not integrated with technical considerations.

Often implementors omit human and people issues in their plans, thinking these issues will automatically be confronted. It's usually not the case. We once visited an organization about to implement a new type of automation in a manufacturing plant. At a planning meeting, when the implementors went over a checklist of human factors that the organization should examine more closely, a personnel representative declared these were factors that "any living person knows and is sensitive to." We pointed out that our research shows these factors are the issues that differentiate what successful people actually *do* when introducing change, as opposed to what those who are less successful *do*. Some months later, we met the production director who talked about "several people" crises that had engulfed the plant. The union had been given limited information about the change (a substantive mistake in a heavily unionized plant), and was now calling for a strike. The shop-floor people were confused and refusing to cooperate. A key technical person had left for another company, leaving the implementation months behind schedule. The omission of human factors from change plans blinded implementors to the critical barriers to progress.

## CHANGE EFFORTS HAVE THEIR OWN LIFE

For most general management interventions, some version of the five stages presented earlier suffice. However, complex change projects often have multiple cycling or iterations of the management process. For example, the following *project life history* shown in Figure 7-3 describes the typical stages of a change project.

**Figure 7-3.  A Project Life History.**

1.  Idea Formulation Stage

2.  Feasibility Exploration Stage

3.  Project Proposal Stage

4.  Design Specification Stage

5.  Test or Model Development Stage

6.  Pilot Test and Review Stage

7.  Full Development Stage

8.  Project Revision Stage

9.  Implementation Stage

10.  Evaluation and Revision Stage

Effective change leaders view the conventional stages in the life span of a change project as a series of agendas. During each separate agenda, they *gather information, diagnose vulnerabilities,* and *solve problems* and *refine plans.* They use the practices of the best change leaders to drive the *content* of the agendas and strategies for overcoming barriers.

In practice, leaders ensure that the human and organizational change elements are included in the change process by stage III (project proposal stage) of the project life history model. Vulnerabilities uncovered become vital design considerations in stage IV. In fact, design specification should address these barriers to change by this phase.

Stages V through VII—the test or model development stage, pilot test and review stage, and full development stage— provide change leaders with vehicles for confronting issues raised earlier. If they are not addressed during these phases, the full development of later stages will be significantly impaired.

When change leaders envision change in terms of the project's life history, they can focus on handling the inevitable human and organizational issues in discrete phases.

## FORMING GOOD HABITS

*Successful leaders make sure they implement change as a continuing process* that encompasses the stages of the project life history. The change does not end with a single master plan. Leaders modify and change plans as their teams gain further insight and specific tasks have been completed. If the specific tasks are not to be repeated, then new tasks take their place. In addition, some problems have to be deferred for solving later in the change process, some strategies do not work, and some cause unforeseen problems. Ongoing planning is the rule, not the exception.

*Change leaders' roles in planned change extend well beyond the phase of implementation.* As they give attention to the change project well after the final implementation, they support change as both a cultural value and a means of personal growth. In addition, the communication feedback and networking so vital for a specific project can become *a per-*

*manent part of the management repertoire.* An organization used an MIS task force to spearhead the installation of a new data processing system. After this first implementation, they kept the group together to monitor systems policy in other areas. The task force quickly established a track record for monitoring the details of systems policy, including whether the systems continued to perform and whether the obstacles to the change were met effectively. It proved so cost effective to have the task force available to review systems that they became part of the full-time staff.

Change leaders often formulate strategies for implementation that develop their organization. For instance, many initiatives to facilitate a single planned change become part of ongoing practices, such as periodic team meetings to clarify plans and processes; larger organizational meetings with top management or other segments of the business to discuss vulnerabilities and opportunities; performance appraisals and project audits; consultant feedback about barriers to change and possible solutions; and permanent involvement of end users to ensure lasting benefits from the change.

*The best change leaders develop planning as a strategic initiative.* Therefore, they use change plans to cultivate the habit of thinking about directions, goals, and beneficial activities. Once team members have formed this habit, future changes become increasingly easy. Members of the change team not only become *trained* to go through the steps of implementation in an organized way, but also begin to adopt information-gathering, problem-solving, and strategy-generating techniques as a way of life, adding new vitality to the organization. As one leader expressed it, "We don't grow stale and obsolete, because we formed the habit of generating plans and goals with specific outcomes. We are constantly creating change without having to drum up some dramatic event! You begin to see change as fun, as a real competitive edge that you can master, rather than something you've got to do just to survive."

## MAKE IT PERSONAL

*The master plan* is a comprehensive document to specify the essentials necessary for a successful change effort. To determine vulnerabilities in planning, you should ask yourself the following questions:

1. Have you had a concrete plan for each phase of your change?

2. Have you modified and adjusted the plan as goals and objectives are expanded?

3. Have you made the plan into a vehicle of influence and motivation for your team?

4. Have you built in a means of accountability for your team?

5. Does your plan provide for effective information-gathering, problem-solving, and goal-setting?

6. Are your goals easy to understand, specific, realistic, attainable, and results oriented?

7. Are your goals timebound with specific milestones and deadlines?

8. Have you communicated the outcomes you expect?

9. Have you gathered the resources to accomplish the steps in your plan?

10. Have you followed the prescribed leadership steps?

11. Does your plan reflect the project life history stages necessary for implementation, evaluation, and revision?

12. Are there gaps in your plan? If so, how do you feel these can be filled?

13. Do you have specfic measures for tracking progress?

14.   Have you arranged for continual feedback?

15.   Do you have provisions for reviewing and evaluating the plan when the project is over to generate ideas for new change plans?

# CHAPTER 8

# Becoming a Change Leader

*Today's and tomorrow's leaders must embrace
change as a value to be nurtured in themselves
and their organizations.*

## IT'S AS SIMPLE AS ONE-TWO-THREE

The principles described in this book have been directed largely toward the good of the organization. Change projects become business successes when individuals implement small, specific strategies that have significant bearing on day-to-day operations.

We have highlighted how confronting three major issues facilitates the introduction of change:

- Preparing your organization;
- Selecting the right people to work on the change effort; and
- Ensuring an adequate implementation process.

These central issues not only correspond to the critical stages of planned change, but in a different form, represent the major

151

personal responsibilities of all change leaders. They are generally *motivated* through the behaviors embodied in preparing organizations for change. They *generate resources* through ensuring that the six roles—inventor, entrepreneur, integrator, technical expert, manager, and sponsor—are covered during the change effort. They *make things work* through the strategies that support the implementation process.

## MAKING CHANGE PERSONAL

One change leader stated clearly that "it is ultimate hypocrisy to demand of your organization things you won't do yourself, but changing yourself is absolutely one of the hardest things on earth to do." Habits from childhood are deeply embedded. Vested interests in certain attitudes and values get in the way of modifying behavior. And often the motivation to change is absent. Ministers, rabbis, and priests will confess that they can couch inspirational messages in sermons to exhalt congregations to change, but they seem to have just as much trouble as most people changing their own behavior.

Fortunately, by demonstrating effective behaviors and making effective plans during a change effort, you've already changed—at least on the surface, and at least for the time of the project. Even more heartening, the strategies described in this book can be applied as well to personal development as they can to an organization. As with any planned change, the first task is to define the arena in which you can have the most impact with change. If you are a top manager, it is natural to think of your entire organization as the domain of change. If you are a systems analyst, your role in overall technical change is more clearly limited. No matter what arena you operate in, every member of an organization can become a change leader. You can start by defining what can be changed and improved in your own sphere of influence and then decide on your strongest role for a change effort.

In preparing yourself for change, you need to ask yourself questions similar to those used for organizational change. For example, you need to *review your personal history of change.* Do you find it useful to change? Do you like exploring new avenues? Are you constantly seeking self-improvement? If so, then some of the steps toward change will be natural—you will *want* to accomplish them. You should particularly review your successes. When you face change, do you tend to "bite off more than you can chew"? If so, you should review and utilize appropriate strategies for the implementation process and spend extra time planning.

In an honest self-appraisal, you may recognize that you resist change because of anxiety or fear of failure. As with organizations, you can probably confront emotional barriers by limiting the size of the change or by breaking it into phases or small steps. Each of these measures will help you tailor the scale, scope, and pace of personal change.

Developing a vision of how you want to be can aid change efforts too. This is the personal parallel to the organizational question—"whose problem are we solving?" Again, the focus should be on clarifying the differences between present reality and the ideal state you're trying to achieve. Individuals who are best at producing personal change focus on reducing the discrepancy between where they are now and where they would like to be in the *future*. Those most successful at personal growth and skill acquisition also use their inner dialogue to highlight specific steps or stages for decreasing the variables between present and ideal performance.

Sometimes individuals undermine success by pursuing personal goals that conflict with their personality style or natural talents. In contrast, those most effective at self-generated change select goals compatible with their past and present life. Perhaps the best way to develop competent behaviors is to select a few practices from the best change leaders. (See those at the end of this chapter taken from the core of this book.) Commit yourself to a small development project, focusing on those vulnerabilities that most interfere with your successes.

Once you have prepared yourself for change, you should *look closely at your resources.* Just as you need to select the right people in an organizational setting as allies and teammates, you need to ascertain your personal assets for change. These include internal resources in the form of opportunities, friends, mentors, allies, and networks.

Many people can provide vital help in the change process. Just admitting publicly that you plan a change is a step that will increase the probability of your reaching your change goals. Building in steps that others can observe and about which they can give you constructive feedback will also help you achieve your objectives.

In the process of taking an inventory of resources you should review the change model roles and dimensions discussed in Chapter 6. Which role do you naturally play? Which role should you be playing in your organizational setting? Which roles are not covered on your own "personal change team"? If you wish to master a new role, choose one that has practices you can easily learn to display. However, don't be afraid to seek counsel from others who are competent at skills you are learning. They can provide helpful coaching tips and cogent feedback about your performance.

Individuals who are effecting complete personal change projects implement plans for change with the same considerations as implementing change in organizations. In order to do this, they *clarify plans* based on goals of moderate risk and milestones they can easily meet. In addition, they apply the same considerations about planning, discussed in Chapter 7, to their personal project plan.

*Clarify your plans.* Make your plans moderate in risk. Develop recognizable milestones that you can easily meet. The same considerations about planning, discussed in Chapter 7, apply to your personal project plan.

*Integrate new practices gradually.* When most people try to change behavior, they tend to fail at first. You will find it easier to develop new practices in easy increments. If you decide to be an expert public speaker, it is probably not a good idea to practice your new-found skill in a presentation to the management of your major customer. You better start at your son's wedding. Even if you fail, most people will only remember your son as a handsome groom.

*Obtain training.* There are many ways to acquire new skills, depending on how you learn best. If you learn well from structured courses, select some recommended ones. For example, to improve your skills in planning, you can attend a project-planning course, or to improve organizational communication, you can attend a communications seminar. On the other hand, you may prefer independent self-study. If so, read or use recognized self-improvement tools. You may prefer to learn through on-the-job experiences. If you become involved in this kind of training, choose a situation where you can try out new skills with relatively low risk. Build in time before you enter the situation to determine what you want to accomplish. Assess your performance immediately after the experience and make adjustments. For example, one of our clients, who frequently had to conduct large meetings with people from a variety of departments in her firm, wished to increase her skills at managing a group. She laid out some specific practices that she felt would help her and used whatever group settings she could find to refine her skills. She began with her own staff meetings where she felt relatively comfortable and even tried out the behaviors with a youth group she led on weekends.

*Obtain feedback from others about how you are doing.* This is important, if you want to make ongoing changes. For instance, just as you would ask different groups for feedback about the rationale for the change, you may want to ask individuals in these groups if they have seen improvements since you began your personal change. Ask them for specific suggestions.

*Measure your successes.* You need concrete evidence that you are succeeding at change. Your plans should be constructed so that you know how you are going to *measure* your success. It is well documented that embracing some general goal, such as "losing weight," is generally of little use. It is much more effective to specify a goal, such as losing ten pounds by Thanksgiving, and then follow through by honoring your commitment and vigorously rewarding yourself if you drop off the ten pounds. We have emphasized how "success breeds success." We might add that "setting up measureable success starts to make success a habit."

It is obvious that incorporating these practices into your own life makes you *a human change model*—a person who has the leadership qualities that your team will eagerly follow. In fact, emulating you will often become part of their personal goals. You will be a true change leader, because you've become a "changed leader."

## MAKE YOUR ORGANIZATION INTO A CHANGE LEADER

Change leadership requires success, not only in individual change efforts, but also in developing an *ethic of change*. First of all, by introducing change according to the principles outlined in this book, your organization will be more successful at initiating any type of planned change. However, the best leaders make change an organizational value by modeling, teaching, reinforcing, and refining the princples of the change model in all day-to-day operations.

*Change leaders devote as much time to dealing with human and organizational issues as with technical issues.* This finding applies especially to technical change. Even though *human* and *organizational* factors are often greeted with skepticism by technical personnel, you must be able to focus on these issues consistently to produce ongoing changes. Some leaders hold special meetings just to discuss the human vulnerabilities that typically derail change. Counteract the tendency to downgrade people problems and support the attitude that people problems in the change must be addressed first.

We have consulted on a number of mergers and acquisitions. We have seen some excellent business plans for the combined businesses. We have heard elaborate discussions about initial communications. We have observed task forces retreat, red-eyed, after discussions of benefit plans and outplacement schemes. But we rarely see an intensive plan to deal with human and organizational issues. Yet, these are the issues that usually determine whether or not the new type of organization will have additional value.

Those who lead mergers and acquisitions are not alone in failing to provide serious planning around human and organizational concerns. If you want your organization to succeed with change, you should *make problem solving the norm*. Some managers hate facing problems so much that they cut off useful information from others about how to solve them. A large technical organization was about to embark on a new technology that some senior managers believed would enable them to open up new markets. They presented it to the chairman, who became very excited about the new technology. In fact, the project became known as the "chairman's project." He was even out selling the technology himself! The only problem was that there were some severe technical limitations in the project, not to mention human resource problems. But it was the "chairman's project" and no one wanted to deal with the problems—until too late!

*Allow information to flow freely, so that problems can be solved.* Check your organization's practices to ensure that there are no major blocks to the passing on of information that could be critical in problem solving. Communication is the responsibility of every leader or potential leader in the organization. Some people in the middle of organizations complain about lack of direction from above. Effective change leaders create their own direction if it is lacking. They gather information to ensure that they are not too far off track and they check their own practices to ensure that they are not a block in a communication chain.

*The change leader who puts vision into practice will be tomorrow's "hero".* When we compare some of the most successful change stories with those that are average or less successful, we find that competent change leaders consistently focus on the final target, constantly looking for opportunities, or confront traps and pitfalls, and are repeatedly developing strategies to avoid them. Many organizations concentrate on bottom-line results and short-term "fixes" to an extent that undermines creative, long-term growth.

By following the practices that we have found that distinguish successful from less successful change efforts, organizations can be significantly more effective at introducing individual changes. However, the most significant benefits of change leadership stem from *developing* individuals, teams, and entire organizations.

We live in a world where nature's way is change. We are accustomed to changing seasons, changing tides and changing moons. For a few people, these natural changes alter their mood or personality. But these changes are not as cataclysmic to people as purely human changes, which seem to send whole organizations into a frenzy. If we are to grow personally, we have to keep changing as individuals. If our businesses are to be competitive, they must remain open to change. If our country is to remain healthy, it must change too. These are important missions worthwhile for each of us.

## MAKE IT PERSONAL

*How clear are your expectations and commitments to what you want to change?* If you cannot classify what to change and why, then your effort will probably fail. Review the following best change practices using the questions below to guide your self-assessment:

- Which behaviors do you demonstrate frequently?
- Which behaviors do you demonstrate rarely?
- Are these important to change for personal or professional success?
- What will be the consequence of changing these?
- Will you improve your performance? If not, then what other practices will help you change?

## ORGANIZATIONAL READINESS

1. By providing, *History of Change,* a change leader
   - Informs end users fully, avoids surprises.
   - Makes a reasonable case for change in end users' terms.
   - Spends more time talking.
   - Involves end users in diagnosing vulnerabilities.
   - Starts implementation with receptive workers.
   - Starts implementation with a small part of the change for quick, visible payoff.
   - Publicizes successes.

2. By providing *Clarity of Expectations,* a change leader
   - Emphasizes the benefits of change—to the organization, the unit, and end users.
   - Avoids surprises; specifies possible impact, outcomes, and problems.
   - Makes change plans public.
   - Solicits formal and informal feedback.

3. By defining the *Origin of the Problem,* a change leader
   * Specifies who wants the change and why.
   * Clarifies end users' concerns about the change.
   * Specifies the effects of the change on day-to-day operations and work routines.
   * Presents potential problems clearly and completely.
   * Sets goals that confront end-user problems first.
   * Uses feedback as a barometer of how fast to proceed with implementation plans.

4. By providing *Support of Top Management,* a change leader
   * Defines top-management concerns.
   * Develops an influence network—top management allies, informal coalitions.
   * Implements a small part of the change for quick results and good publicity.
   * Develops a formal management review from top management's perspective.

5. By demonstrating the *Compatibility of Change,* a change leader
   * Frames the change in terms of present organizational values and goals.
   * Integrates the change into ongoing procedures when possible.
   * Makes change plans overt, common knowledge.
   * Starts the change in an accepting environment.
   * Doesn't oversell the change.

## CHANGE-TEAM ROLES

1. *Inventor*
   * Makes a wide search for change suggestions.
   * Reviews the common organizational and social sources of the innovation.
   * Talks about potential future problems.
   * Discusses the what-if implications of new technologies, market changes, etc.

- Uses the team to review products and services periodically.

2. *Entrepreneur*
   - Works on tolerating partial answers, interim solutions, mistakes.
   - Practices framing ideas so that they "sell."
   - Develops change resources and influence networks.
   - Develops planning and goal-setting skills.

3. *Integrator*
   - Develops interpersonal skills.
   - Develops informal alliances and coalitions, as well as a formal team.
   - Protects the change project from the usual organizational pressures.
   - Confronts conflicts and clarifies distortions.
   - Informs and updates key personnel.

4. *Expert*
   - Acquires knowledge and skills, or is responsible for finding experts.
   - Develops skill of working with "outside" consultant(s).
   - Develops presentation skills.
   - Updates team members and end users.
   - Monitors change plans.

5. *Manager*
   - Develops coaching skills.
   - Sets goals skillfully.
   - Specifies, reviews, and revises change plans.
   - Delegates responsibility freely.
   - Takes responsibility for outcomes.
   - Keeps morale high with frequent face-to-face feedback.

6. *Sponsor*
   - Seeks support and resources from the highest levels of the organization.

- Interprets the purposes of the change to top management.
- Communicates where the change fits in the overall organizational vision.

## THE IMPLEMENTATION PROCESS

1. *Clarifying Plans*
   - Makes one person responsible for implementation plans.
   - Formulates clear, simple, timebound goals.
   - Makes specific plans with milestones and outcomes.
   - Makes plans public.
   - Gives and solicits frequent face-to-face feedback.

2. *Integrating New Practices*
   - Limits the amount of change introduced at any one time.
   - Slows the change process.
   - Introduces the change to receptive users first.
   - Ensures that the rationale and procedures for change are well known.

3. *Providing Education*
   - Involves the end users and incorporates their experience.
   - Provides hands-on training whenever possible.
   - Designs training from end users' perspective.
   - Trains motivated or key end users first.
   - Evaluates the effects of training on work practices and end-user attitudes.

4. *Fostering Ownership*
   - Ensures that the change improves end users' ability to accomplish work.
   - Provides incentives for end users applying the change.
   - Specifies milestones for getting end-user feedback.
   - Incorporates end-user suggestions in the implementation plans.
   - Publicizes end-user suggestions.

5. *Giving Feedback*
   - Documents and communicates the expected outcomes of the change.
   - Ensures frequent face-to-face feedback.
   - Identifies clear milestones.
   - Makes sure feedback includes the entire organization.
   - Acknowledges key successes.

# Index